Architectural Guide
Tel Aviv

Architectural Guide Tel Aviv

Sharon Golan Yaron

Research assistant and co-author:
Yuval Even

DOM publishers

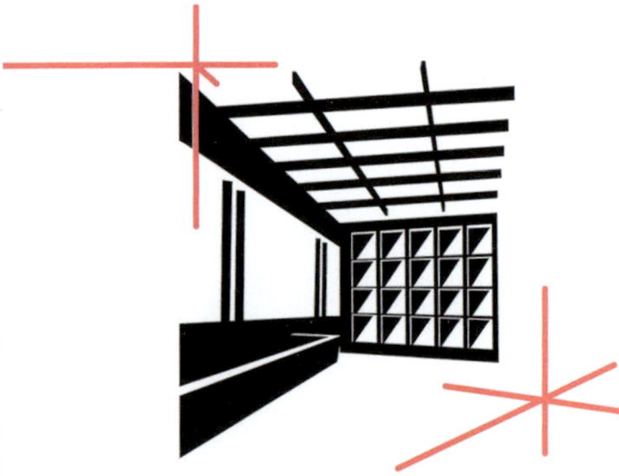

The entrance hall then and now
The way home starts here

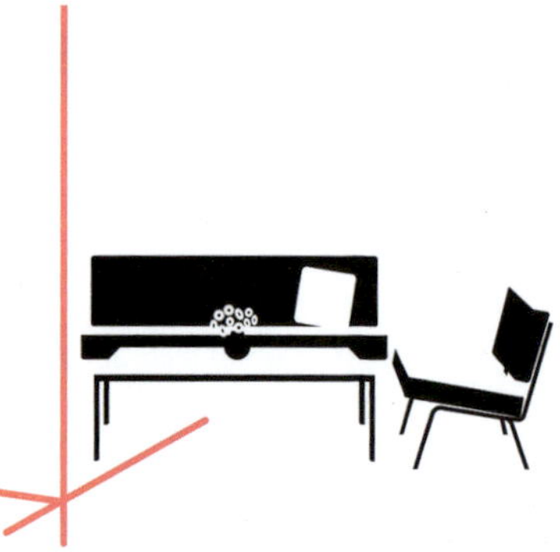

The living room
The discipline of the vitrine

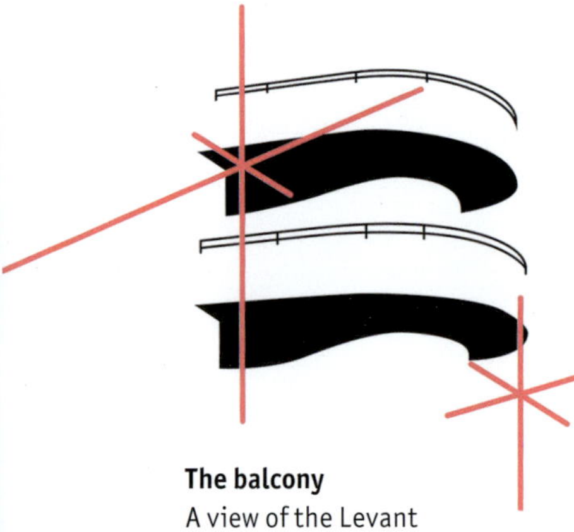

The balcony
A view of the Levant

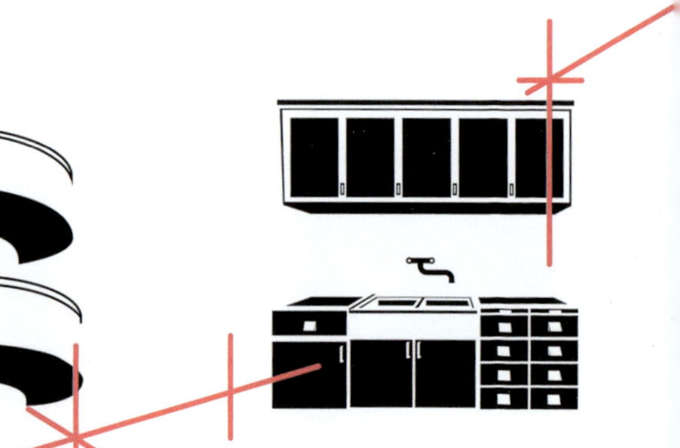

The kitchen
From modernism to post-feminism

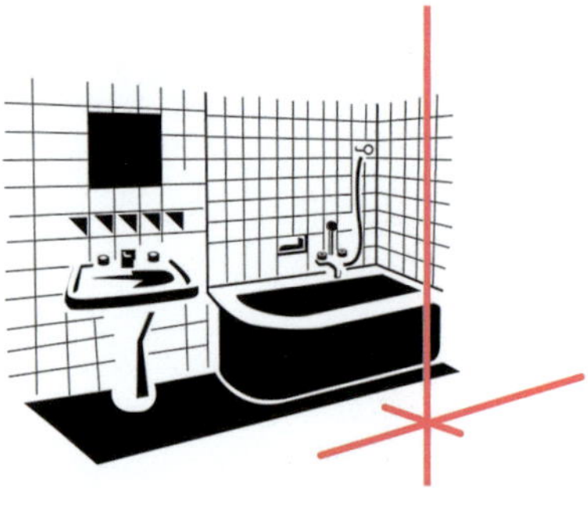

The bathroom
Ceramic or porcelain

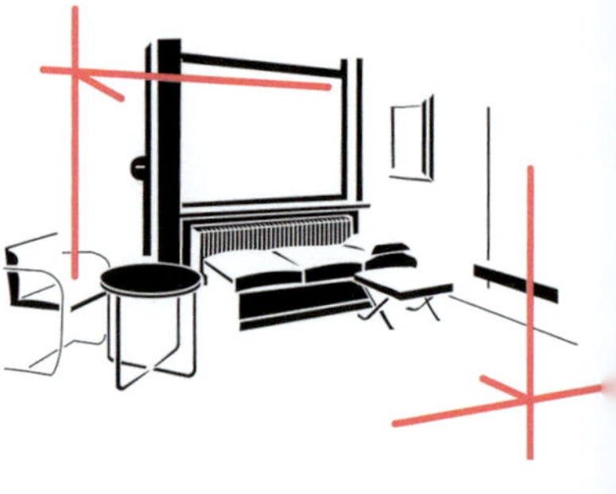

The bedroom
From Schlafstunde to power nap

Typical architectural elements of The White City

About this Book

We chose to publish this book on the occasion of the centennial celebration of the Bauhaus school, the Avantgarde school that had such a lasting effect on building in the twentieth century. The book presents 100 buildings along various routes through Tel Aviv's urban landscape. Although Tel Aviv's architecture cannot be referred to as a purist Bauhaus style, it was certainly deeply influenced by the school. So much so that in 2003, the White City was declared as a UNESCO World Cultural Heritage site due to its outstanding cultural significance of the various trends of the Modern Movement in architecture and town planning in the early part of the 20th century. A distinction that comprises more than the Bauhaus Style buildings alone.

The selection of 100 buildings for this architectural guide along the four chosen routes was challenging. The number of buildings constructed during the 1930s is very large, and during the selection process we were constantly finding ourselves eliminating some and adding others; choosing a limited number was difficult to do. Tel Aviv has no outstanding icons, no recognised stand-alone architectural masterpieces that could by themselves define its unique style. Rather, what makes the White City so special is its historical urban landscape, which extends far beyond the declared UNESCO site. Therefore, we chose to devote one of the tours to the outskirts, the fringe, and included buildings that are not officially declared architectural monuments. Tel Aviv is a living, evolving urban fabric that rose from sandy dunes in the beginning of the twentieth century. It was created by thousands of immigrants from all over the world, creating a melting pot of cultures cast into the concrete silhouette of buildings of the so-called International Style.

Because any selection of buildings can only be an arbitrary sample representing just part of the Modernisms built in the city, we urge our readers to continue discovering their very own version of Tel Aviv, with their favourite buildings and the spaces between them. Walk inside the buildings' front gardens, and peak into the lobbies to discover the impressive richness of shape and form. Choose your own special spots and pause once in a while for a cup of coffee in one of the little kiosks or visit the small shops. We hope that with this tour guidebook one can learn to understand and appreciate the characteristics of Modernism in Tel Aviv, even in places where, at first glance, neglected and deteriorating façades coin the image of the streets. Learn to read the proportions of the buildings, even if the balconies are closed off with aluminium and plastic shutters. Discover the arrangement of the building ensembles, even if neglected front gardens have been turned into improvised parking lots. Sometimes, patina and traces of historical substance are far more intriguing than a perfectly renovated building. This is the moment to discover Tel Aviv's historic, social and cultural fabric. Here, the presence is always a moment right before dramatic change takes place. Because this city is constantly changing.

Sharon Golan Yaron

iStock (purplexsu)
045
Rothschild Boulevard
Nachmani Street

Bird's-eye view of Tel Aviv's historic heart

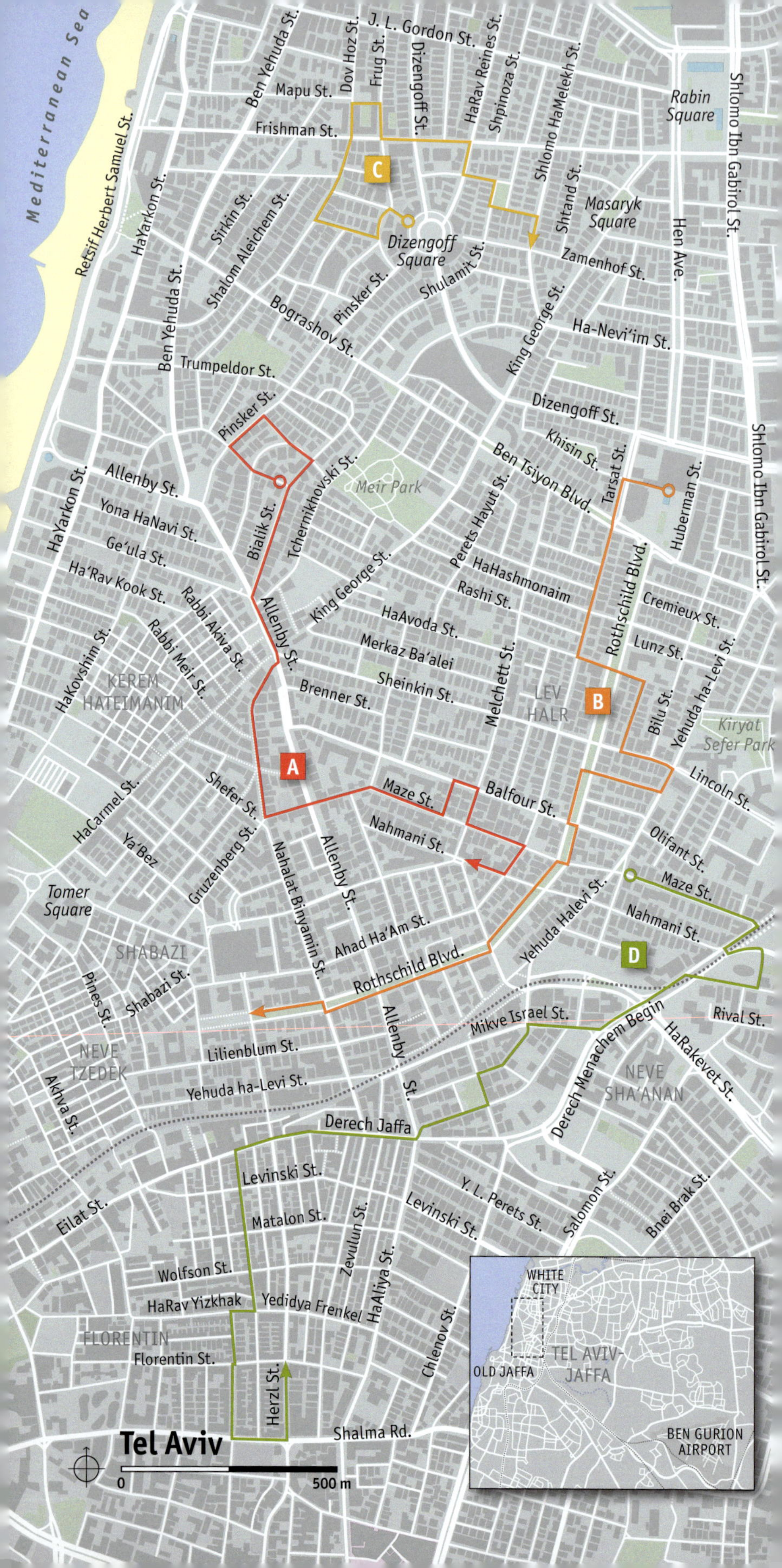
Tel Aviv
Mediterranean Sea
Rabin Square
Masaryk Square
Dizengoff Square
Meir Park
Kerem HaTeimanim
Lev Ha'ir
Kiryat Sefer Park
Tomer Square
Shabazi
Neve Tzedek
Neve Sha'anan
Florentin
A
B
C
D
0
500 m
White City
Old Jaffa
Tel Aviv-Jaffa
Ben Gurion Airport

Contents

Karmi Archive

Max-Liebling House, 29 Idelson Street, Architect: Dov Karmi

Central part of Tel Aviv looking down on Allenby Street, 1932

Library of Congress

Introduction to the White City

More than just Bauhaus

Upon entering the city of Tel Aviv from the Ayalon Highway, one is struck by skyscrapers that lunge at the sky from inbetween a colourful forest of cranes. This freeway marks the edge of something that resembles a giant bathtub forming around the heart of Tel Aviv's historic old town. The White City, a 10-hectare large UNESCO world heritage site in the city centre, threatens to become engulfed by a development frenzy.

Tel Aviv prides itself on being a global city, a city that never sleeps. Its duality is due to the contrast of the prevailing historic heart and the constantly developing fringes, between the efforts of conserving the existing structures while simultaneously erecting new buildings, sometimes right on top of the historic buildings. While on street level, historic layers are being frozen in time or restored to their former glory, a few storeys higher, a completely new layer is being added to the city, forcing the pedestrian to conceive it from a worm's-eye view.

This urban development lies at the base of the local conservation approach, the result of the pressure to reconcile conserving significant historical cultural attributes of the city with allowing for much needed new development. In the process, the century-old city tries to adapt to the frenzied contemporary lifestyle of Israel as a start-up nation.

Yael Schmidt

View from the White City onto high-rise constructions at the beach promenade of Tel Aviv

The onset of the twentieth century and how it all began

When looking at the first map drawn of the area where Tel Aviv is located today, one mainly detects sand dunes along the Mediterranean Sea shore, a few scattered houses built by Palestinian settlers, and the Templer settlement. The Templers were German Protestants belonging to the Pietist Movement. They believed in the apocalyptic visions of the prophets of Israel in the Holy Land. From the middle of the nineteenth century onward, they emigrated to Ottoman Palestine in order to found communities in Haifa, Jerusalem and Jaffa, among other places.

The Templers constructed their first settlements just north of the Port of Jaffa. These German settlers possessed excellent farming skills which they had developed specifically for their life in Palestine. They focused mainly on the implementation of orange groves and wine plantations. Both of these goods were exported and led the Templers to economic prosperity. The local Shamouti orange was particularly valuable as its thick skin allowed for a longer shelf life, thus making it particularly suitable for export. Hence, the Jaffa orange became a well-known brand, which can still be found in European supermarkets today.

The Templer settlement had an immense influence on the later development of the city as, in the beginning of the twentieth century, the inhabitants of the small Jewish community of Jaffa imitated the skilled German settlement both in terms of agricultural and architectural planning.

The first Jewish settlement outside the walls of Jaffa, called Ahuzat Bayit was built in 1909. It symbolised the gate to the new Jewish town in Palestine, like, according to its founder Akiva Arieh Weiss, New York to America. The new settlement was built in the shape of a cross; with the important difference to other Templer settlements being that in the new Jewish settlement the Gymnasium, instead of the town hall, was located at the crown of the vertical axis, symbolysing the importance of education for the community. Later, this same Herzliya Gymnasium, a Hebrew high-school, turned into the symbol of the local conservation movement. When it was destructed in 1965 in order to be replaced by the new Shalom Tower (the first high-rise construction in the Middle East), the dismay about the loss of this historical icon resulted in fierce criticism, which ultimately led to the establishment of the National Monument Preservation Council that is still active today.

The once small settlement outside the walls of Jaffa has now grown into a large city neighbourhood. The former one to two-storey-high, red roofed suburban houses turned into two to three-storey high buildings built in the so-called Eclectic style.

This began at the start of the 1920s and lasted until about 1928, when a large immigration wave mainly from Eastern

Zoltan Kluger

Beach Promenade, landscape architect: Avraham Karavan, 1938

Europe swept the country. The style can be best described as an assemblage of a neoclassical European style, British colonial architecture and different decorative elements according to the architects' individual taste. With the help of European building technology, motifs of the local Levantine surroundings were blended with Jewish motifs: the balustrades with their iron railings, for example, were adorned with oriental domes, pointy horseshoe arches, wooden oriels and biblical motifs. Examples can be found in the shape of a menorah (Jewish candle holder) or biblical drawings on decorative tiles and glass work. In general, the Eclectic style was rather a search for a local language using manifold ornaments rather than a clearly definable style.

So-called dream homes became the highlights of this style; with rich homeowners extravagantly displaying their financial situation on the façade. One such example is the Pagoda House, in which all styles were mixed together with each floor featuring a different building style, all topped off with a steel Pagoda roof.

Through the connection between Orient and Occident, the architects of the Eclectic Style wanted to develop a regional-national architectural style that would reflect the intertwining of Judaism and the Levant with European culture. The search for a national architectural style ended, however, in stagnation and architectural confusion. Criticism arose claiming that Tel Aviv had become a provincial European city, 'Little Warsaw' or 'Little Odessa'. Nevertheless, it became noticeable that the first signs of a new architectural style laid the path for the language of modernisms. The appropriate academic term for the architectural style of Tel Aviv is 'International Style', a term used for a global modern style coined by Philip C. Johnson and Henry-Russell Hitchcock in 1932 on the occasion of an exhibition at the Museum of Modern Art (MoMa) in New York. It stands for the attempt to use architecture as a unifying act of globalism. The international form of the buildings represented a contemporary approach of design. Especially in Tel Aviv, the style expressed the desire of the newly founded city to be as modern as possible. At the same time, it strove to create a new environment as a counterpoint to the old building traditions predominant in the home countries of the refugees and to the local vernacular architectural style of the Levant.

Albeit, the term Bauhaus became part of the everyday language to describe the buildings of the International Style in Tel Aviv, undoubtedly expressing the desire to be able to use a catchy slogan for the local building style. To adorn the city with the glory of Bauhaus as a realised social utopia, and to sell an ordinary, so-called Bauhaus apartment with a 25 per cent markup.

Yet, the architecture of the city is far more complex than the term Bauhaus allows for. It combines many different views and modernisms of European imprint, based on a whole slew of protagonists. Coined by many influences, Tel Aviv has created its own global language while accommodating the climatic and cultural conditions of the first Hebrew city.

The Garden City plan

Almost parallel to the adaptation of modernism, just five years earlier, another outstanding event of lasting cultural significance had occurred. The British mandate, which ruled Palestine until the foundation of the State of Israel in 1948, introduced the idea of the Garden City to Israel, a concept formulated by Ebenezer Howard in 1898 in England as a remedy for the harsh conditions in European towns following the industrial revolution.

Master plan by Sir Patrick Geddes, 1925

In Tel Aviv, this idea of a garden city provided the urban context for the individual, freestanding architectural objects of the White City.

In 1925, Scottish urban planner Patrick Geddes, one of the foremost theorists in the early modern period, was commissioned by the British mandate to implement British theories in new town planning. Geddes, a biologist, sociologist, geographer, philanthropist and town planner, proposed turning Tel Aviv into a garden city. With his environmental approach and his insight into the nature of the city as an organism constantly changing in time and space, he developed a plan of small land plots and freestanding buildings. One guiding principle was to let light and air into the houses and the sea breeze blow through the streets. The road system was organized according to a hierarchy of main traffic axes, residential streets and footpaths.

The ideal block he designed was to be built as a 200-metre-long, 200-metre-wide square with four main ways that

Municipal Archive

Tel Aviv's city park typology

extend beyond the block and form a part of the large street network. The long north-south streets were designed to be commercial streets combining commerce on the ground floor and three to four residential storeys above them with the traffic lane. The block itself was divided by four secondary blocks that are not contiguous and connect to each other at T-junctions. The streets were deliberately cut off to keep the interior of the block quieter. The area between these four streets included a public garden or a local communal building.

In an attempt to create an optimal residential density for the city, Geddes defined the layout of the lots according to a number of principles: the typical plot area is about half a dunam (around 500 square metres), ending four metres away from the curb and around three metres from the adjacent building, ensuring a distance of six metres between one building and another.

Thus, creating spaces for vegetation and allowing the sea breeze to flow between the buildings. His visionary plan, laid out between 1927 and 1929, determined the main characteristics of the city and defined the relationship between the structures and their surroundings, between the residents and their environment.

Geddes' original design for the new Tel Aviv was more than just an urban masterplan. It was supposed to become a political, social and cultural tool to help create the New Jew in an ideal habitat. This human engineering was a core part of those parts of the Zionist movement who dreamt of recreating a proud Maccabean nation. They believed that this aim could be achieved by resettling emigrants from the confines of Eastern Europe's ghettos in a healthy, verdant garden city; a place which would provide a healthy environment, fulfilling their needs both physically and spiritually. No one could have imagined that this new Hebrew city outside the walls of the old port city of Jaffa would experience massive growth in such a short period of time.

Following the Nazi's ascent to power in 1933, 250,000 Jewish refugees from Europe fled to Palestine. Only two decades had passed since the foundation of Tel Aviv. Within a few years, Tel Aviv's population tripled, rendering many of Geddes' original designs obsolete.

Modernity and modernisms

Erected by tens of thousands of emigrants from all over the world, Tel Aviv is a melting pot of cultures cast into the concrete silhouette of buildings in the so-called International style. At the same time, Tel Aviv has no outstanding icons, no unique architectural Bauhaus masterpiece that in itself could define the style of the city. Rather, what awards the White City outstanding cultural significance is the fusion of the buildings with their urban context, the historical urban landscape, which extends far beyond the boundaries of the declared UNESCO zone with its numerous listed buildings. It is a continuously developing, living, evolving urban tissue that rose from sandy dunes by the sea at the dawn of the twentieth century, and should be read as such.

The main construction phase of modernity in Tel Aviv lasted only about six years, from 1931 to 1937. It was the heyday of the International Style and the Bauhaus movement. The influence of the interwar architecture in Europe and new, local developments led to multifaceted modernistic interpretations. They reflect the needs of the society and culture by adjusting the International Style to the local constraints of climatic conditions such as the harsh sunlight and the existing building material in Palestine. The latter was easy to work with, for example silicate bricks, bricks that were used as filling in concrete

Stadtarchiv Stuttgart

Icon of Modernity: Weissenhof Estate in Stuttgart, shortly after the opening in 1927

frame constructions and allowed the inexperienced Jewish building workers to enter the labour market.

The most predominant group shaping Tel Aviv were young architects which had left Palestine earlier to train as architects and engineers abroad. They had studied in Germany, France, Belgium, Italy and Russia in the workshops of the most famous architects of the Avantgarde. Arieh Sharon, Shmuel Mestechkin, Shlomo Bernstein, Munio Gitai Weinraub, and Chanan Frenkel studied at the Bauhaus. Josef Neufeld was trained in Rome, Bruno Taut in Moscow, Ze'ev Rechter by Erich Mendelsohn in Berlin, Shmuel Barkai by Le Corbusier in Paris. Dov Karmi, Benjamin Ankstein, Genia Averbuch, as well as many others, studied in Rome, Gent, Venice or Naples, later also in Vienna and Paris.

Many of them were to become key architects in the future state of Israel. They were driven by the modernistic ideologies of the current Zeitgeist, and their wish was to cast their creative guidelines in concrete in the newly formed state.

Around 1930, modernity was the answer for all building projects. However, the first modernistic building in Palestine, a hydroelectric power plant, was designed by Berlin architect Erich Mendelsohn already in 1923. Modern architecture was now realigned ideologically and stylistically to identify possible solutions for the Zionist enterprise. As agents of a proactive, pragmatic Zionism, the members of Chug supported the Zionism of Theodor Herzl with his social aspects. While Modernism thus got a new push in Palestine, the so-called *Neues Bauen* ('new building') in Germany was banned and rejected as 'Jewish-Bolshevist' and 'Semitic oriental', like in the case of the Weissenhof Estate in Stuttgart.

In order to educate the public as well as to invite tenders for architectural competitions, Chug published a magazine called Habinyan Bamizrach Hakarov (Building in the Near East). It promoted innovative ideas such as building on *Piloti* ('columns') to allow the breeze to circulate through the streets and buildings. Garden passageways underneath the building structures were to subtly connect the buildings to the street. Semi-public, shaded entrances often adorned with fountains, pergolas, and benches led to the building lobbies.

The Chug group succeeded in changing the aesthetic standards of the Yishuv, the community of Zionist Jews that had begun to settle in Palestine since the end of the nineteenth century. Their modernistic language was appropriated by the Zionist movement, it became the architectural expression of the desire to create a new national identity. Thus, Modernism came to symbolize the birth of the new Hebrew nation.

Stadtarchiv Stuttgart

Antisemitic propaganda: Weissenhof Estate as an Arab village, postcard 1940

This intimate connection between the Chug and the socialist leadership of the Yishuv helped institutionalise modern architecture, which goes a long way to explain the almost homogenous appearance of Tel Aviv's city centre.

It did not harm that the uniform and relatively sober style of Modernism facilitated putting roofs over the hundreds of thousands people flocking to Palestine in the 1930s as part of an unprecedented wave of refugees. Erecting houses with reinforced-concrete frames was less time-consuming and expensive than the Eclectic Style with its load-bearing walls and lush ornaments. The solutions and building concepts developed by the architects of the Avantgarde in Europe proved to be suitable for Palestine, too, and were therefore willingly adopted.

The predominant building material, limestone bricks, was easy to produce locally and did not require any special crafting skills. The modern construction method allowed greater wall openings, projecting balconies, and a flexible arrangement of the interior spaces. Terrazzo was cast on-site with local and imported stones. Plaster was made with the newest technologies brought in from Germany and applied in situ with various techniques. The use of artificial stone products by mixing minerals such as lime and white cement with various small stones and grain gradations lent the façades a three-dimensional appearance and made them particularly resistant.

A German engineer called Emanuel Teiner came to Palestine specifically to train Jewish construction workers, teaching them how to create the different types of plaster common in Germany at that time: exposed aggreagate plaster, scratched plaster and stone plaster. The best proof for the strong influence of German building techniques on the country is the Hebrew language. Many of the German terms are still being used by Israeli workers to the present day, along with other words such as *Sockel* ('plinth'), *Oberkante* ('upper edge'), *Unterkante* ('lower edge'), *Stecker* ('plug') or *Unterputz* ('rendering').

However, Jewish refugees from Germany imported more than just know-how with them. In 1933, the Zionist Federation of Germany negotiated the terms for the so-called Haavara Agreement with the Ministry of Economics of the German Reich. Jews wanting to leave the country, who were otherwise denied access to their liquid funds in fear of the *Reichsmarkflucht* ('Reich Flight Tax') could now transfer part of their cash assets to Palestine. Furthermore, there was a growing boycott of German goods by the Americans.

The Zionist Federation of Germany saw the Nazi government's fear of another recession as an opportunity to sign an agreement with the Nazis, the Transfer

Transfer Agreement, 1938

Agreement (1933–1938). This was a controversial episode in the relationship between Israel and Germany, which remained obscure despite the fundamental impact it had on the Jewish settlement in Palestine.

German Jews paid their money into a transfer bank, for which the Tel Aviv-based company Haavara then purchased machines, construction material and other wares in Germany and sold them in Palestine. Upon their arrival, the emigrants received the proceeds minus accrued expenses.

Whereas the nationalist socialist government considered the emigration of Jews a stroke of luck and saw the agreement as a means to gain foreign currency gains in view of the international financial boycotts, more than 50,000 Jews successfully fled Germany in 1939 during the onset of World War II, and therewith certain death in a concentration camp. Their cumulative wealth amounted to 150 million Reichsmark. Some of the transferred materials were trivial daily ware such as socks, buttons, cocoa-powder, matches, mason's trowels, or football shoes. Yet, a huge amount of other materials was used to construct the buildings that make up the White City, such as tiles, glass windows, handles, fixtures, metal and concrete. Longing for the European lifestyle they associated with their roots, immigrants used these goods to try and maintain their identity, while, at the same time, demonstrating knowledge about the latest trends of architectural design. Although only six of the architects who later designed buildings in Tel Aviv actually studied at the Bauhaus, the influence of this small group on the architectural discourse in the city was immense. An example can be seen at the Hod Cooperative Housing Estate on Frishman Street completed in 1935: the influence of Hannes Meyer, the second and somewhat lesser known Bauhaus director, can be discerned here, both in the simple and modest design form and in the social

Tel Aviv street view with kiosk, 1909

Hannes Meyer, 1929

structure of the building. Residents were allocated only small apartments but shared huge communal facilities including a large garden in the centre of the estate, a common kindergarten, a laundry, shops and a dining hall. In keeping with the socialist worldview of the ruling elite, these communal public spaces served as an extension of the relatively small living units, with the task of welding the new Hebrew society together into one homogenous whole.

This directly corresponded with the teachings of the architect and urbanist Hannes Meyer. Meyer was known as the 'socialist' director of the Bauhaus, coining slogans like *Volksbedarf statt Luxsusbedarf* ('the needs of the people instead of the need for luxury') and directing his students to focus on the social aspects of design as their main agenda.

Arieh Sharon, who held Diploma No. 6 of the Bauhaus in Dessau, was to become Israel's most prominent Bauhaus architect. Coming to study at the Bauhaus from Kibbutz Gan Shmuel, where he had already worked in planning and construction, one can imagine the immediate connection he managed to form with his master Meyer, trying together to translate socialism's ideals into architectural forms. It can even be argued that the student may have influenced his teacher, one example being the ADGB Trade Union School in Bernau/Berlin.

The ADGB, a masterpiece recognised as a UNESCO world heritage site in 2017, embodies many formal spatial attributes representing direct parallels to the kibbutz settlement in both form and function. In both, the space was arranged to guide the communal behaviour of its inhabitants, ranging from small residential rooms to semi-public spaces, all the way to the large communal gathering spaces such as the dining hall – all to help shape the identity of the individual as part of the group.

Sharon's most important work, however, was accomplished a decade later, after the high days of early Modernism in Palestine. In 1949, he was commissioned by the first Prime Minister of Israel, David Ben-Gurion, to lead the team that was to design the first masterplan for the newly established state.

This plan was published in 1951 under the term 'Physical planning in Israel', determining the location for new towns in the country and laying down the principles of regional planning in order to distribute the large influx of immigrants. It regulated the location of industrial areas and agriculture zones, the general infrastructure system as well as national parks and nature reserves. So, it would not be an exaggeration to state that a Bauhaus student not only designed the residential buildings in Tel Aviv, but actually laid out the strategic masterplan for the whole country of Israel.

In retrospect, his design has been much criticised. But establishing settlement developments in the periphery of a city to house poor immigrants, which unfortunately quickly turned into social hotspots perpetuating the differences between Israel's upper and lower classes, was not what Sharon had intended. Much rather, Sharon applied well-known and established planning practices, inspired by a model developed by German geographer and economist Walter Kristaller. During the last decades of his life, Sharon designed a masterplan for the University of Ife, Nigeria, whose agenda includes integrating local artistic motifs in Modernist buildings.

Escaping from the National Socialist regime in Germany, and following the occupational ban of Jewish architects, some 60 architects came to Palestine until 1934, among them such illustrious names as Erich Mendelsohn, Adolf Rading, who followed his Jewish wife to Palestine, Julius Posener, Leo Adler, Oskar Kaufmann, and many others.

Most of these architects chose to immigrate to Palestine not because of a deep ideological Zionist conviction, but rather because they found a professional incentive in the underdeveloped country and saw a chance to work there.

Many of these architects, who already were established architects in their homeland, were forced by municipal city engineer Yaakov Shifman to adopt the International Style which he had mandated for all new constructions. Oppositional impulses led to the development of very individual forms of Modernism, among which more expressive forms of *Sachlichkeit* (Objectivity). And not all architects entirely abstained from using ornaments even if Modernism held high the dictum postulated by Adolf Loos 'Ornament is crime'.

The development of Israel's local style was never a simple copy of European know-how. Rather, it represents an evolution of a unique local language in the functional doctrine of Modernism, reflecting the needs of a nation in the process of coming into existence. It is based on the values of the Zionist movement as well as on the fundamental needs of a new country that had to take on more than a million immigrants constantly flocking to the country.

Perhaps the most predominant feature of the local adaptation of the International Style is the relationship between the buildings and the streetscape, as it was already determined in the Garden City plan. The buildings are individual, detached monoliths on their respective plots, allowing the growth of vegetation on all four sides. They stand in constant dialogue with their surroundings, offering perpetual social interactions between occupants and passers-by. The raised *Piloti* houses (an idea adopted from Le Corbusier) offer a gradual passage from the public sphere into semi-public, lush gardens, while creating pleasant micro climatic conditions on hot summer days.

The balconies with their various types of appearance are another dominant feature of Tel Aviv's urban fabric. Whereas modernistic buildings in Central Europe feature small or introverted balconies on the rear façade, the balconies in Israel serve as shading as well as holding a social function.

Tel Aviv's inhabitants have always interacted from their balconies, creating a vibrant street atmosphere by connecting the dwellers with the passengers on the street, and the balconies serve as the main means of communication between neighbours. Usually acting as an outdoor extension to the living room, most of the balconies are shaded and ventilated. The only vertical window element, the so-called thermometer window, also facilitates the dialogue with the street, as it not only lets natural light penetrate the stairway during the day, but also illuminates the street at night time with artificial light.

The UNESCO declaration

In 2003, Tel Aviv was declared a UNESCO world heritage site due to its outstanding cultural significance of the various trends of the Modern Movement in architecture and town planning in the early part of the twentieth century. It is considered the largest urban concentration of the International Style worldwide. All in all, there are 3,700 International Style buildings in Tel Aviv, 1,000 of which were selected for preservation. In total, 190 buildings are subject to stringent monument protection.

The UNESCO declaration led to the implantation of a conservation plan that was created in order to restore the built fabric of the city. The starting point for the creation of the plan was the need for the city to grow because of its evergrowing population, while, at the same time, keeping in mind the desire to conserve the nature of its historic heart.

Most buildings in Tel Aviv are privately owned, the conservation regulations are designed to enable homeowners to afford the relatively high cost of the conservation process by granting additional building rights on the rooftops of their buildings. The proceeds from such additional spaces can be used to cover the cost of renovation.

In practice, approved building permits mean that three storeys can be added to

Installation of a giant construction worker at the *Levant Fair*, 1937

a building. This involves concrete obligations on the side of the owner: they are not only required to adhere to stringent renovation codes but must ensure earthquake resistance and add rocket-safe shelter rooms, preferably in the form of a shaft in the rear area of the building that remains invisible from the front of the building.

Together with UNESCO, a system of Transferring Development Rights (TDR) was authorized in 2003, permitting to transfer the building code requirements from buildings listed under strict preservation regulations (the 190 buildings mentioned above) to different projects, which, in practice, meant that the building rights could be sold. Again, the money gained from such sales of building rights could be used to offset the cost for the preservation of a historic building even if it was listed under the stringent conservation code.

When planning building additions for buildings listed as historical monuments, the task of the architect is anything but easy. They have to keep in mind that modernist architecture attached immense importance to the proportions of the

overall building. Up to three additional storeys are added to many buildings, which sometimes doubles their height. If the addition is built in the same style as the original building, the delicate relationship between horizontal and vertical proportions are in danger of being lost.
Merely imitating the original style would also make it impossible to distinguish between the original building and a new addition. If, on the other hand, all new additions would be created in an entirely different architectural style, this 'upper city' would soon dominate and overwhelm the historical buildings on the lower level. Since every building in Tel Aviv has its unique character, the original proportions of the building as well as its particular position on the plot must be carefully analysed to understand its essence – the key for designing suitable extensions.
A number of preservation purists will certainly raise their brows at the addition process described above. But the City of Tel Aviv bravely defies the enormous pressure that real estate giants impose on it by relegating high-rises to areas outside of the historic heritage zone. It pays a high price for trying to maintain its historic centre: investors are suing the city for 2.5 billion US dollar as compensation for the loss of real estate value. Tel Aviv must respond to the needs of the modern State of Israel, the country with the highest growth rate among all OECD states. Even if the new urban masterplan has numerous issues, it does offer carefully elaborated solutions for today's constraints and necessities.
Israel is a young country, having only just celebrated its 71st anniversary, but is still fighting for its existence. To many, preserving its heritage, especially that of modernism (which not everyone finds aesthetically pleasing) seems like a luxury, particularly in light of the existential threats that the country faces.
Nonetheless, the conservation plan upholds Patrick Geddes' unique ideas and the proportions of the modern city, while allowing for renewal and new development. Unfortunately, the heart of the city does not have the privilege of becoming a museum of architecture; rather, it has to continue to serve as the living tissue of Israel's most important metropolis, which keeps on growing and needs to keep adapting to the demands of the contemporary society.

The White City Centre

In 2015, in cooperation with the German Federal Ministry of the Interior, Building

Yael Schmidt

Max-Liebling House: Staircase during the *Open for Renovation* Project

and Community, the City of Tel Aviv created the White City Centre to preserve the historic heritage of the White City. This holistic approach is the local answer to the management plan of the declared UNESCO heritage site of Tel Aviv, considering the urban ensemble as connected to all layers of the city while taking into account the socio-economic aspects of the growing metropolis.

The White City Centre is situated in Max-Liebling House, a typical modernistic building in the heart of the city. Designed as a residential building by architect Dov Karmi in 1936, Max-Liebig House is also listed as a monument. The centre serves as the central contact point for all issues related to the world cultural heritage. It will house a visitor information facility with a small café and a shop, a community garden, a research facility, a space for workshops, a residency program and a space for changing, contemporary exhibitions dealing with aspects of monument preservation in a broader context. The official opening of the centre will take place on the occasion of the centenary celebrations of the Bauhaus in September 2019. The opening will include bilateral exhibitions and international events dealing with cultural heritage and urban development as well as offering a professional fellowship programme. With the White City Centre, the city wants to contribute to fulfilling the management plan of the UNESCO world cultural heritage declaration and, not least, raise awareness of Tel Aviv's interesting urban landscape, which is naturally a little more complex than a single Bauhaus icon could ever be.

Open for renovation Project *Bauhütte*

While it was undergoing renovation work, Max-Liebling House, the future White City Centre, became a venue for live performances, a showcase window, and a laboratory all in one, exposing the layers of the building, its conservation process, and traditional handicrafts, while promoting a better understanding of the values of modernist architecture. This meant that Max-Liebling House was open during the renovation and invited the public to visit its rooms in a series of lectures, tours, and art shows that offered new perspectives on the building and the city. There was a monthly public programme was devoted to the different sections of the house and included a real-time *Bauhütte* (real-time working site) for professional exchange in the field of conservation.

Holzer Kobler Architekturen

Holzer Kobler Architekturen: Competition design for Max-Liebling House (2016)

The Historic Heart

Barak Brinker

Barak Brinker

Bialik Square: Modernism and More

Tel Aviv's historic heart beats at Bialik Square. This urban square was named after the Israeli national poet Hayim Nahman Bialik, whose home was located here. The area of the square holds architectural treasures that were designed between the 1920s and the 1940s by leading architects of the time; it is a showcase for the ground-breaking Israeli architecture of that period. The buildings in this area are of historical, cultural and municipal importance.

This tour will take you to one of the most important heritage sites of Tel Aviv – the buildings in this area are of historical, cultural and municipal importance, and give the complex a unique character. The tour will start at the Max-Liebling House, which houses the White City Centre and serves as the central contact point for anything concerning the White City. Max-Liebling House includes numerous exhibitions and events dealing with the heritage of the White City and with the contemporary development of the city in general, an ideal place of introduction to the topic of the tours. The Bilalik Square itself is one of the most important heritage sites of Tel Aviv, around it there are numerous cultural public sites, such as the former municipality which was turned into an art gallery, the Bialik House, the Reouven House, and the privately owned Bauhaus Museum, which are all open to the public.

In 1922, the "Bialik Commune" settled on top of a desolate hill, now the highest hill of Tel Aviv, the so-called Bezalel

Bialik Square in a 360 -degree panorama shot

Hill. They were among the first settlers to come to the country as part of the third wave of Zionist immigration. The commune set up a small tent camp and adopted a communal lifestyle. Both men and women worked in construction and laid roads. The group remained intact until 1924, by which time Hayim Nahman Bialik, Israel's national poet, had also immigrated. One would like to imagine him joining the others in their singing and dancing in the evenings. Most of the homes built during the 1920s were designed as single-storey villas in the Eclectic Style.

Within just a few years, Bialik Street had become an upscale neighbourhood where artists, writers and especially renowned physicians took up residence. Apart from the house at 19 Bialik Street, all these imposing houses were later torn down and replaced with two- and three-storey buildings, some of which representing the International Style.

Bialik Street ends at the east side of Allenby Street, one of the city's main traffic arteries, which provides a direct connection to the seashore and the city's main market.

The tour passes along Allenby Street which reflects the architectural and planning history of the city. All of the city's major construction periods are represented in this area. Unlike in the White City further north, there is no separation between the quiet residential neighbourhoods and the crowded public streets.

Max-Liebling House **001 A**

29 Idelson Street
[A] Dov Karmi, Eng.Zvi Barak
[R] Rivka Karmi under the office of Ada Karmi in collaboration with Yohntan Cohen and Dan Hasson
1936

This building is one of the 190 buildings listed as a monument under the most stringent preservation codes. It has been chosen to house the White City Centre, which functions as the hub for all matters concerning the conservation of Tel Aviv's declared UNESCO world cultural heritage site. Designed by Dov Karmi and Engineer Zvi Barak, this free-standing structure is an icon of Modernism. It is perfectly situated on the plot in order to maximize the sea breeze coming from the western shore. The building's composition emphasises functionality. In order to make good use of the irregular site, the building was composed of two main blocks (facing toward the front and the rear of the plot) holding three storeys each. The stairwell in the centre serves as a hinge connecting the two columes. On each level, the front and the rear block are also connected by a continuous service balcony, which is accessible from both of the apartments located on each storey. The front volume, with an almost square footprint, is situated parallel to the street. The central part of the street façade stands out as a rectangular shallow relief, creating an overall frame and a counterpoint to the three deeply recessed balconies whose horizontal emphasis determines their character. The arrangement of the windows and the layout of the floorplan

promote the flow of air into the building to cool and ventilate the living rooms. The long and narrow balconies of the façade, a local adaptation of Le Corbusier's strip windows, function as a second skin in front of the actual building envelope, shading the living spaces behind them while providing an interface between the private and the public spheres. The pergola of the entryway connects the two blocks using a concrete ring beam that wraps around the corner of the building. The entryway through the vegetated pergola passes along a goldfish pond, which contributes to the cooling effect. Labour-saving devices in the kitchens, bathrooms, and on the balconies as well as up-to-date technical equipment demonstrate the commitment to a functionally and economically well-thought-out design. Examples of such installations like the "Frankfurt Kitchen" on the second floor are open to the public. The building was an upscale residence, serving as a home for three prominent physicians who emigrated from Central Europe. The architects had originally built Max-Liebling House for real estate manager Max Liebling and his wife Tony. In 1963, ownership of the building was transferred to the municipality of Tel Aviv, with the wish to establish a museum, kindergarten or student housing. To learn more about the origins and the early days of the city, about Modernism and the International Style in Tel Aviv, as well as about the houses of former, highly acclaimed residents and their architects, visit the White City Centre and its exhibitions, and walk all the way to the roof to see the city map drawn out there.

Yael Schmidt, 2018

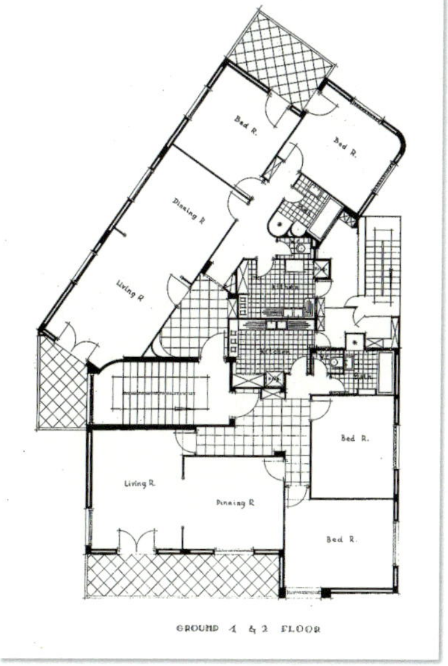

Municipal Archive

Itzhak Kalter/Karmi Archive

House Kruskal I

002 A

25 Idelson Street
[A] Richard Kauffmann
1931

House Kruskal I, the first International Style building built in Tel-Aviv and still standing today, was designed by Richard Kauffmann, one of the country's leading architects. The house was designed as a town villa for the family of Dr. Kruskal, who also operated a private clinic on the ground floor. In 1935, a third floor, with a floorplan identical to that of the second floor, was added by architect Selman Selmanagić, a Muslim of Bosnian descent, who worked at the Kauffmann office. The floorplan of House Kruskal I was designed within the boundaries of a perfect square with rectangular subtractions that soften the massiveness of the composition. House Kruskal I was the first in the city to integrate the use of wide, cantilevered canopies as a climatic solution. Prior to House Kruskal, the use of such constructions was strictly decorative. The dimensions of the protruding roof areas were directly derived from the angles of the sunlight in order to prevent direct sunlight penetration during summertime yet allowing it to enter in winter. The building is characterised by strong horizontal lines on the dark-coloured, rustic plaster façade. The plaster area originally included horizontal stripes on the ground floor, as well, which were later removed. Up until today the building serves as an urban family villa and holds local Israeli sculptures in its well-maintained garden.

Itzhak Kalter

Denis Esakov

Philipp Meuser

House Kruskal II

003 A

23 Idelson Street
[A] Richard Kauffmann
1934

In the case of House Kruskal II, the building's highlight is to be found at the rear façade, which features an impressive, curved concrete emergency stairway accessible form Idelson Street. The staircase embodies the virtuosity of both the architect and the craftsman in dealing with the new building materials of the 1930s. The building was commissioned by the same family as the adjacent House Kruskal I, and designed by the same German architect, Richard Kauffmann. This building is characterised by a distinctively symmetrical floor plan. The façade facing Pinsker Street is split by the entrance leading to the building's staircase, which creates two mirroring fields. The façade facing Idelson Street is composed of two volumes, each featuring alternate horizontal emphasis techniques - its western volume is equipped with ribbon balconies, while the eastern part features wide cornices. Over the years, the ribbon balconies were closed with aluminium windows, which serverly diminished the building's original quality.

Philipp Meuser

***Menshalach*, Little people in Yiddish – Metal holdings for wooden shutters with a female face on one side and a male face on the other, the urban legend refers to them as the secret code between the city's lovers. When the female side was up it was a signal that the coast is clear, inviting the lover in.**

Denis Esakov

Philipp Meuser

House Mintz-Elenberg
Beit Ha'Ogen

004 A

23 Pinsker Street
[A] Pinchas (Philip) Hütt
1935

Itzhak Kalter, 1936

Originally planned as a residence for young women, this house is a result of the extensive number of immigrants arriving in Palestine during the fifth immigration wave, created a housing shortage that had to be answered by extending the built fabric. The majority of new buildings contained apartments with two or three rooms and were meant to accommodate families. But many of the young immigrants could not afford to pay the high rent prices, and therefore rented rooms in family apartments. However, renting a room to young, single women was not customary. As demand kept rising, brothers Heinrich and Gottfried Mintz along with their business partner Heinrich Elenberg commissioned architect Pinchas Hütt to design a pension for young women. Hütt designed a three-storey building of communal fashion, containing small residential units, fitted to one person, along with communal areas such as a kitchen, a laundry room, and a living room. Each apartment was composed of a room with an adjoining bathroom and a toilet. Access to the apartments was granted by long corridors stretching across the entire length of the building. Long indoor balconies served as a connection between the living units on each side of the building. The building is composed of a long, rectangular and symmetrical volume determined by the parcel's shape. The façade's most prominant features are the thermometer window composed of glass and metal bars, the still original glass entrance door, and black tiles that act as an anchor for the buildings vertical mass. Over the years, the building's program was neglected, the communal areas were turned into apartments, and the balconies were closed in order to expand the living unit's area.

Philipp Meuser

House Efraim Strod

005 A

1 Brock Street
[A] Victor Jakhon
[R] Nira Reichman Architects
1934

Built originally as a three-storey structure, the footprint of House Efraim Strod follows an L-shape which generates a courtyard on the street corner. Its two volumes intersect at the building's entrance, above which lies the circulation core. An impressive, rounded thermometer window emphasises the building's corner. The building was renovated in 2009. The renovation included the addition of an extra three storeys on top of the original building. What became the fourth floor follows the original floorplan, while the fifth and sixth floors are recessed progressively to make them less visible from the street. Although the renovation reinstalled the building's original vitality, the added storeys changed the overall building's proportions. The original façade was extended upwards in order to grant the building a coherent appeal.

Philipp Meuser

Philipp Meuser

Philipp Meuser

Philipp Meuser

House Joffe 006 A

21 Bialik Street
[A] Shlomo Gepstein
[R] Nachum Cohen
1933

House Joffe is a white cubic building that replaced a one-storey urban villa built in the Eclectic Style, which was located on the same plot but was demolished in 1933. Russian Architect Shlomo Gepstein, who studied in Saint Petersburg, designed more than twenty residential buildings in Tel Aviv, mostly in the International Style. Even though House Joffe was intended for residential purposes it actually served many different functions throughout its lifetime. Esteemed local architects such as Sam Barkay, who served as the building inspector for the Bialik House across the street, and Ze'ev Rechter operated their studio from one of its apartments. House Joffe is located on a corner plot in proximity to the former city hall and, for some time, housed municipal offices until it was remodelled to accommodate municipal dental clinics. In 1995, the building was purchased by Roland Lauder and Daniella Luxembourg, who turned it into a museum dedicated to the Bauhaus in Tel Aviv. Although the renovation in 1998 aimed at returning the building to its original design, the ground floor was modified to include a public space, and the window frames were changed.

Philipp Meuser

House Pelzmann

007 A

18 Bialik Street
[A] Eliyahu, Emanuel Friedman
1934-1935

This residential building was built on a plot formerly occupied by a one-storey Eclectic style building. The former building was built in 1927 as a house to Dr. Eliyahu Berlin, one of Tel-Aviv's original founders. Each floor of the new L-shaped house, built from 1934 to 1935, is composed of two five-room apartments and a four-room apartment. The building features a large garden made possible by a recess in the building volume. Although the garden was much changed over the years one can still see traces of the limestone that used to border the flower beds. The rounded protrusion on the recessed building volume allows westerly breezes to flow into the apartments oriented toward the north. The façades facing the streets are also characterised by rounded corners. The streamlined shape of the building was probably influenced by German architect Erich Mendelsohn. The thermometer windows of the building feature an opening mechanism that resembles that of the Bauhaus in Dessau. Also noteworthy is the original exposed aggregate plaster.

Denis Esakov

Irmel Kamp-Bandau

View from Sapir Café towards the Mediterranean Sea

Philipp Meuser

House Mintz - Café Sapir

008 A

2 Bialik Street
[A] Shmuel Dov Chaim Kriss, Eng. David Tuvia
1932

This one-storey commercial building used to house Café Sapir, one of Tel-Aviv's first cafés, reflecting the newly imported coffee house culture which was brought to the Levant by the "Jekkes", the German Jews of the fifth immigration, along with their favoured Goethe and Schiller libraries. Café Sapir hosted many of the city's cultural figures. Its location overlooking the sea, and its adjacency to Allenby street, made it an ideal spot for such an establishment. Originally, the building was to be designed in the Eclectic Style, but these plans were shelved after the plot was sold to the Mintz family, who later decided to erect a similar building. The 1930s brought a change in municipal regulation regarding buildings style. Jacov Shiffman, the city engineer at the time, was known for rejecting any Eclectic Style building, hence the Mintz family building was designed to follow the principles of the International Style. As such, the building features a strong horizontal emphasis that is articulated by its wide, cantilevered cornice which stretches across the glass façade, and an elongated façade ribbon above the glass storefront, along with a terrace with an unencumbered view of the sea. The building went through many changes throughout the years since it was no longer used as a café. The main space was separated in order to accommodate a wider array of businesses.

Philipp Meuser

Philipp Meuser

House Shimon Binyan

009 A

56 Allenby Street
[A] Lotte Cohn, Eng. Josef Mahrer
1936

Berlin-born architect Lotte Cohen, who had studied at Technical University Charlottenburg, was the first female architect in Israel. She was not only a pioneer of the architecture in the country, but also became a pioneer in Kibbutz and Moshav architecture after working as a senior architect in Richard Kauffmann's office. This building was originally designed as a U-shaped office building that comprised three storeys. The ground floor housed commerical functions. House Shimon Binyan demonstrated restrained plasticity, the façade is characterised by clean lines. It features openings on the two office floors that create a clear horizontal band, which is bordered by a slightly recessed frame. The original top floor was marked by a horizontal balcony which is designed with stepped, horizontal bands. These bands emphasise the horizontality by use of the play with light and shadow. The building is located on a plot which is bordered by three streets, three of the street façades are almost identical. As befits an office building of that time, it was designed with an impressively generous circulation core and an entry hall accordingly spacious. In 2001, before Tel-Aviv's preservation policy was established, the building was renovated, and two new floors were added behind a brown balustrade, which greatly changed the building's original proportions. A historic photograph of the building is placed in the entrance hall.

Ya'akov Rosner

Philipp Meuser

Philipp Meuser

House Polishuk

010 A

62 Allenby Street
[A] Ya'akov Orenstein, Shlomo Liakovski
[R] Nitza Metzger Szmuk
1934-1936

The 1930s brought a change in Tel-Aviv's built environment. Originally, the city did not include many office spaces and commercial zones because its residents worked in Jaffa, creating a clear separation between living and working areas. The year 1934 marked a shift for Tel-Aviv since it obtained the status of a city. Tel-Aviv became self-sufficient and finally separated from Jaffa. This transformation resulted in the construction of large-scale office buildings in the city centre. House Polishuk was built in one of the city's most bustling locations - Magen David Square, which connects six important arteries. Originally, the building housed commercial spaces on the ground floor, and offices on the upper floors, making it one of the first office buildings in the city centre. The building follows a V-shape. The sharp angle of the V is rounded in order to expand the footprint of the building and to enhance its appearance as an important location in the city. It can be assumed that the architects drew inspiration from Erich Mendelsohn's Schocken Department Store in Berlin. The building was designed with a strong horizontal emphasis, which is articulated by its ribbon windows, elongated balconies, and cantilevered cornices. The cornices' orientation shifts vertically to mark the rounded corner and to tie the roof pergola to the rest of the building. Unlike most of the buildings constructed at the time featuring a plaster finish, this building was clad with ceramic tiles. House Polishuk was refurbished in 2013. One of the aims of the renovation was to transform it into a boutique hotel. Architect Nitza Metzger Szmuk in collaboration with interior designer Qarim Rashid created luxury rooms and a rooftop with a pool and a bar. Taking a break at the rooftop bar overlooking the city all the way to Jaffa is highly recommended.

Denis Esakov

Denis Esakov

Zoltan Kluger

Philipp Meuser

House Gottgold

011 A

51 Allenby Street
[A] Rephael, Yehuda Megidovich
1936

Despite being built on a relatively small plot, this office building's presence is a prominant feature in the cityscape of Tel Aviv. New municipal regulations set in the 1930's specified restrictive building boundaries. Buildings facing the square had to be built at a recess from the street edge and with rounded corners, in order to visually expand the square and creating a coherent image with the adjacent buildings. Today, a dynamic contrast exists between the deteriorated stage of this building and the newly renovated stage of the Polishuk House, its counterpart building on the other side of the street. The staircase of House Gottgold is located on the building's eastern edge, which gives the façade its asymmetrical appearance. The staircase core projects vertically beyond the building volume, and its top section expands horizontally to form a concrete pergola. Like the pergola, the other horizontal elements also originate at the staircase core and expand towards Allenby street, which creates a dynamic flow that ties two streets together.

Denis Esakov

Zoltan Kluger

Philipp Meuser

House She'altial

012 A

3 Nachalat Binyamin Street
[A] Arieh Cohen
1935

House She'altial is a residential building that includes a commercial area on the ground floor. The functions are separated by a cornice that is followed by a continuous window band. The curved windows were made of glass imported from Europe. The apartment apertures are framed by two narrower cornices to enhance the horizontality and grant them a band-window appearance. Those horizontal bands are further accentuated by the contrast between their light, sanded stone cladding and the darker-toned scratch plaster surface of the other areas of the façade. The plot on which the building stands is shaped like a trapezoid, resulting in a sharp-angled corner. The horizontal window bands extend beyond the corner to enhance the façade's dynamic feel and accentuate its perspective.

Philipp Meuser

Philipp Meuser

House Isser Shulmann

013 A

31 Gruzenberg Street
[A] Ben-Ami Shulman
[R] Alon Architects
1938

Isser Shulmann, a merchant from Jaffa, acquired two adjacent plots in 1922 and built a single-storey building on each of them. In 1935, Isser Shulmann commissioned architect Ben-Ami Shulman to design a three-storey office building that was to include commercial functions on the ground floor. He wanted it to be located on the street corner on one of his plots. The architect's original design included a large building with the option to expand it to the adjacent lot. Yet, due to financial restraints in addition to bureaucratic hurdles, the overall building volume was reduced to only include a commercial building on one of the plots, which was composed of a ground floor and a gallery floor above it. The building housed a total of seven shops. In contrast to other buildings erected in Tel Aviv at the time, Shulman incorporated the use of glass as the main building material in his design, with the entire length of the gallery floor featuring a continuous ribbon window. To overcome possible overheating of and through the glass, the

Irmel Kamp-Bandau

windows were slightly recessed in the façade and a concrete canopy provided shading. Another feature distinguishing this building from others was the separation of the façade from the building structure, a characteristic very common within the European modernist movement but not so in Tel Aviv's examples of the style. The building is currently being renovated. It is to be connected to the adjacent plot, and three additional residential floors will be added. With the new additions, the building will resemble the original design from the 1930s, even if it exceeds the dimensions envisioned then.

Philipp Meuser

House Dinitz

014 A

20-22 Gruzenberg Street
[A] Ya'akov Orenstein, Shlomo Liakovski
1937

House Dinitz was erected on a lot formerly occupied by a one-storey building which included commercial functions. The building was designed to include mixed use functions, with commerce occupying the ground floor, and a mixture of office spaces and apartments on the two upper floors. The planners were some of Tel Aviv's leading architects of mixed-use buildings in Tel Aviv. Its location on the irregularly shaped corner plot generated the building's V-shape. The former building extended to the boundaries of the plot, while the current building's edge was recessed and rounded in order to expand the street space and grant fluidity to the street corner. The offices and apartments on the upper floors are accessed via two separate stairways, each facing a different street. The horizontality of the apertures on the building's upper floors is further emphasized by slightly projected concrete canopies that frame the openings.

Philipp Meuser

PHARMACY
Welcome by
durex

Irmel Kamp-Bandau

House Bruno

015 A

3 Strauss Street
[A] Ze'ev (Wilhelm) Heller
[R] Bar-Orian Architects
1935

This building was designed by well-known Leipzig architect Zeev (Wilhelm) Heller who, before immigrating to Israel, had specialised in buildings of decorative expressionism in Germany and Breslau (today part of Poland). Similar to his other buildings, House Bruno exemplifies the possibilities of a double skin concrete façade, separating an inner, private and functional plane from an outer, more public plane with decorative qualities. To overcome the narrow street façade, the building's north-facing façade features a formation of wave-like balcony ribbons that seemingly float along the façade, and a set of balconies located on the north-eastern corner that protrude toward the street. These measures grant the side façade a decorative function and allow more daylight into the building. In 2004, House Bruno was renovated, two additional storeys were built with a recess from the street façade and an additional apartment was added on the ground floor.

Philipp Meuser

House Israeli

12 Maze Street
[A] Yehoshua (Shani) Steinbok
[R] Bar-Orian Architects
1939

016 A

This building shows the shift in building style in the new Jewish city from Eclectic to modernism, resulting in a fusion of them both in the design. Originally conceptualised as one of two building comprising the Ein Gedi Sanatorium, it was built in the 1920s in the then common Eclectic Style. By 1936, after the sanatorium had been abandoned and the building had stood vacant for some time, its function had been changed to a residential building. During the conversion, one storey was added, and the façade was stripped of ornamentation resulting in an apparently modernist building with a symmetrical façade that is not typical of the International Style which typically avoided symmetry as a design principal. In 2010, the building was renovated, another storey was added following the outline of the existing floorplan, plus an additional recessed roof-top penthouse floor. Notice how the architect refined the switch from scratch plaster to a smoother plaster finish by hiding it behind rain drainage pipe.

Itzhak Kalter

Philipp Meuser

Philipp Meuser

Zoltan Kluger

Philipp Meuser

House Magen David Adom

017 A

13 Maze Street
[A] Yaakov Shiffman
[R] Messer Architects
1934

This building was designed for Magen David Adom, a medical first-aid organisation established in 1930 and still operating today. It functioned as the organisation's headquarters until it was converted recently. Its architect, Yaakov Shiffman, was the city architect between the years 1929 and 1950. During his tenure, Shiffman stopped approving plans for construction in the Eclectic Style, the style that had characterised Tel Aviv in its early days. Shiffman took considerable effort to transform Tel Aviv to a city built on modernistic values by implementing strict regulations and forcing planners to build only in a modern architectural language. As befits his post, he designed many of the city's public buildings. The Magen David Adom House is composed of two main building volumes within a horizontal framework and an additional vertical volume that houses the staircase. Its façades are asymmetrical and feature apertures of varying size that relate to the function of the space they permit light into. A few years after its initiation, one additional storey was added to the building. In 2014, it was renovated and converted to function as an extension of the school it neighbours. The existing school building was also designed by Yaakov Shiffman. The renovation included a new ward on the building's western part which is disconnected from the main mass and features different materiality housing the shelter rooms.

Itzhak Kalter

A

House Bijonski

018 A

4 Ein Vered Street
[A] Eng. Pinchas Bijonski
[R] Bar-Orian Architects
1936

House Bijonski was not only designed and owned by Pinchas Bijonski, the architect and his family also resided in one of its apartments. Built on a pedestal, this building was originally composed of a basement with three garages and storage rooms for its residents, and three residential storeys on top. Each of the three upper storeys houses three apartments, the two apartments on the rear side offset from the front apartment by half a floor. The building is shaped like an L to facilitate creating a front yard and wide entrance stairway, both of which are enclosed by a wall made of local sandstone. The building is distinguished for its red coloured metal detailing which emphasise its horizontal and vertical articulations. Between 2000 and 2002, the building underwent renovation including the addition of shelter rooms and three additional storeys. The first additional floor follows the original floorplan while the other two top floors are recessed and covered in smooth white plaster which contrasts the off-white pigment of the building's original exposed aggregate plaster.

Philipp Meuser

Philipp Meuser

Philipp Meuser

House Beiser

019 A

33 Balfour Street
[A] Eng. Mordechai Rosengarten
1935-1936

Itzhak Kalter

This building is distinguished by the wide glass screen separating the building from the street, although this feature is not original since the frames were replaced in the 1980s. House Beiser was built on a relatively large plot almost double the size of most plots in the area. Contrary to other L-shaped buildings constructed at the time that are characterised by a front garden and a recessed façade, in order to fully exploit the area of the lot, the Beiser House's back façade regresses to form a backyard. Two stairwells lead to the upper storeys housing several apartments each. Three of the apartments have three rooms and one apartment is two and a half rooms. Because of the natural height differences in the lot, the basement floor was also used as an apartment. The back stairway is accessed via a narrow bridge which allows light and air to penetrate into the deep-set apartment. As is customary for buildings of that time, the building's façade is bare of any ornamentation, it follows an asymmetrical composition, and features vertically oriented apertures to allow natural lighting of the staircase. Even though the street façade is split in half by the vertical window, and its proportions are equal on both sides, the edges are designed to contrast one another - one side features bulging balconies, and the other sunken balconies, emphasising the fact that the building corners have no load-bearing function. Take note of the original, stylish designed entrance door that completes the vertical excise of the building.

Philipp Meuser

A

Philipp Meuser

Philipp Meuser

Philipp Meuser

House Yeruchalimski 020 A

24-26 Balfour Street

[A] Shlomo Flato

1935

House Yeruchalimski stands out for the design of its entrances that virtually set a stage, from the garden design to the lobbies themselves. Built on two adjoined plots, the building is composed of three rectangular volumes, which are separated by a projecting central building volume that is further emphasized by a grid-like concrete pergola on the roof. The volumes located on either side of the central mass have separate entrances and feature elongated drawer-like balconies. It is recommended to step inside both lobbies since the architect created two very different scenarios. What the two lobbies have in common are their spaciousness, windows made from cast glass and green tiles that were probably imported from German, as well as benches and mirrors. 24 Balfour Street still features the original modernistic font on its number sign and an interior fountain made of the local exposed aggregate plaster. One can see the emphasis the architect put on a meticulously designing a picturesque garden, embellished with lush greenery, and rows of flower beds bordered by local sandstone. 26 Balfour Street has an impressive, Art Deco influenced fountain in the garden made of the same broken tiles used in the lobby. The green garden and its fountain chills the air and creates an outdoor space with a comfortable micro-climate system that allows sitting outside on the hot summer days. A wooden bench in the lobby features custom-made lighting, and the stairwell made of cast terrazzo has small, round windows.

Philipp Meuser

Breinin House

021 A

5 Melchett Street
[A] Pinchas Biezunski
1936

Pinchas Biezunski, an architect belonging to the Freemasons, who has also designed the building on 96 Hayrkon Street which, today, houses the most expensive penthouse in the city, designed this building. Breinin House follows the cluster building typology, and consists of three volumes that form a circulation core at the point where the volumes meet. The building volumes are arranged in an L-shape to improve the exposure of the apartments to the prevailing wind coming from the sea. Adjacent to the inner edge is a front garden. The entrance is accessed through the front yard and the elevated floor area which sits on concrete columns (*piloti*). The *piloti* on the ground floor and the slightly outwards projecting canopy on the building's top tie the three volumes together and grant the overall building volume a coherent appeal. The wall encircling the plot was made with raw, unprocessed local Limestone.

Philipp Meuser

Philipp Meuser

House Elishav

022 A

27 Maze Street
[A] Joseph & Ze'ev Berlin
[R] Hagai Tamir Architects
1931-1932

House Elishav was built in the early 1930s by well-known Russian architect Joseph Berlin, who founded the first architecture schools in Israel. His buildings can be seen as harbingers of the International Style. The early examples of Berlin's designs with their Exclectic Style façades highlight his masterful use of the exposed local silicate brick. In this building, Berlin presents a different and less expressive, decorative approach of using this material. An approach probably influenced by his son whose designs picked up the new concepts of Modernism. The horizontal emphasis of the building's façade is created with horizontal bands made of fair-faced brickwork and contrasting bands covered with a red plaster finish. The polychrome façade marks the stylistic transformation from Art Deco oriented design to the aesthetic principles of the International Style. The building was renovated in 2001, and two additional floors were added.

Philipp Meuser

Municipal Archive

Philipp Meuser

House Barun

38 Maze Street
[A] Zaki Chelouche
1933

023 A

This cluster building was built on a triangular corner plot and presents different façade views depending on the street perspective. The façade facing Ahad Ha'am Street features volumes with orthogonal articulation, while the façade facing Maze street is composed as a cluster of contrasting volumes characterised by rounded and straight edges. Each of the volumes is higher than it is deep or wide, hence the architect integrated a wide variety of elements to accentuate the building's horizontality: elongated cornices, ribbon windows, bulging balconies, and a polychrome finish, amongst others. The building is one of the buildings under strict preservation restrictions and was renovated in 2008 .

Itzhak Kalter

Philipp Meuser

Philipp Meuser

House Romanov

024 A

25 Nachmani Street
[A] Leo Adler
[R] Yoav Messer Architects, Nitza Metzger Szmuk
1925

The design of this house was inspired by the typical Berlin style rental building, with long central corridors. It is the first house in the country planned by architect and architectural critic Leo Adler. Originally, the building was designed for his wife's family who had emigrated to Palestine in 1925, while he and his wife stayed in Berlin. The building represents the first attempt to build in the Art Deco Style in Tel Aviv. The façades are void of ornaments, except for beam-shaped cornices above and to the sides of the windows, designed to shade the rooms and keep away the harsh direct sunlight. This feature gave the building its nickname, The Falling House. House Romanov was also the first building in the city using scrolling shutters in all the windows on the main façades, contrary to the Eclectic Style buildings that had hinged shutters influenced by the local Arab building tradition. The building is also completely exceptional in its conceptual approach of "form follows function" as it tries to solve the climatic challenges of the Levant through architecture. In 1933, eight years after his father-in-law had settled in, Adler was arrested by the Nazi authorities for his cultural activities. He decided to take the warning sign and emigrate to Israel, where he moved into the house he had designed. After an elaborate renovation in 2012, the building has turned into a luxurious boutique hotel with an added recessed floor of suits and an infinity pool on the roof. The hotel has an exclusive range of well-recommended restaurants.

Sivan Askavo

Spring in Palestine – The Spielberg Archive

Sivan Askayo

Sivan Askayo

Courtesy of the Department of Special Collections, Stanford Libraries

House Shimshi

025 A

48 Montefiori Street
[A] Dov Hershkovich, Ram Karmi, Simone Friedman
1933/2000

Originally built on a triangular plot facing King Albert Square as a residential building, this post-modern building demonstrates the approach of conservation in the early 1990s in Israel. The history of House Shimshi exemplifies the problematic issues with cultural heritage preservation in Israel. Ram Karmi, the architect of the post-modern successor building, chose to largely dismantle the existing building in order to erect the new office building he was commissioned for. Even though Nitza Metzger Szmuk, former head of the conservation department (at the time of the UNESCO world cultural heritage declaration in 2003) demanded that the original building be kept, Karmi created a new interpretation leaving only the exterior façade in place. The completely new interior, which shines through the apertures of the original façade, embodies a second glass façade and a glass elevator as attractions. The elevator is the core design element. It is designed in the shape of a waterfall – an homage to the historic water tower of the neighbourhood which is very nearby. A protective metal screen was added to parts of the façade which incorporates the shape of the sycamore tree standing next to the plot, casting its shadow on the building. It is recommended to take a look inside the building to fully grasp the relationship between the old building and its new representation.

Philipp Meuser

Philipp Meuser

The Vibrant Boulevard

View east onto Park Avenue from Rothschild Avenue, around 1946

Library of Congress

Philipp Meuser

Michael Shubitz

Rothschild Boulevard, view from Habima Square to the south

Rothschild Boulevard and its Surroundings

The vibrant Rothschild Boulevard is the city's main artery, leading up to its cultural heart at Habima Square. The boulevard played a key role in the urban development of Tel Aviv, featuring sites and buildings where major historical events took place, including the Declaration of the Establishment of the State of Israel. Rothschild Boulevard is one of the first four streets in Tel Aviv that were paved over dunes in the neighbourhood of Ahuzat Bayit. The sand dunes were straightened, flattened, and paved before the first houses of the city were built upon them. The path that later became the avenue was a small *wadi* (a river creak), which had been difficult to straighten at the time and also drained too much water during winter. As a result, it was decided to fill it with sand, leaving it as an open area on which no houses would be built. Thus, the street became a garden boulevard.

Habima Square at the northern tip of the Boulevard connects the city's main axes. A ring of boulevards surrounds the square: Rothschild Boulevard, Chen Boulevard, Ben-Gurion Boulevard, and Dizengoff Street. In 2007, a garden sculpture was added to the square created by artist Dani Karavan, well-known for his memorial sites around the world. Also added was a huge parking garage that can serve as a shelter room in case of emergency.

On our tour along the boulevard, one can detect the chronologic evolution of architecture in Tel Aviv. From Eclecticism to International Style to Brutalism - it tells the story of its geographical, social, and cultural formation, from south to north, all the way to the cultural Habima Square, where the cultural palace Heichal HaTarbut (Charles Brondman Auditorium) marks the transition to the Brutalist Style of late Modernism which became the dominant style shortly after the establishment of the state in 1948.

Today, the boulevard is home to Israel's start-up scene, where listed buildings adjoin skyscrapers, and historical conservation is the backdrop of the city's continuous development.

Do not miss stopping along the way and sip a cup of coffee in one of the oldest kiosks of Tel Aviv.

< **Rothschild Boulevard: a traffic artery for electric scooters**

Yakov Garden

026 B

Habima Square-
Between the Habima
Theatre and the Mann Auditorium
[A] Architect Yaakov Rechter
with landscape architect Avraham Karavan
[R] TAMA Architects
by Lital Szmuk Fabian
1964

Public awareness for the heritage of the city began to form at the exact spot that, according to Patrick Geddes' Garden City Plan, the cultural acropolis of Tel Aviv was to be built. When the area was ready for the construction of the planned Tel Aviv Museum, the townspeople began to vehemently fight for the sycamore trees that stood on the land. The result was that this garden was specifically created to keep three ancient sycamore trees, which are so typical for Tel Aviv. The conflict became part of the collective memory; so much so that there are songs written about the sycamores of Tel Aviv which became part of the urban landscape, expressing its nostalgic value. Ironically, the trees also cause immense damage to the façades of the White City as their fruit attracts bats which spit the shell of the fruit onto the buildings, leaving dark brown stains on the white plaster.

Instead of the planned museum, the Helena Rubinstein Pavilion was built,

serving as an extension to what is the Tel Aviv Museum today. The museum proper was eventually built in the northern part of the city. Yakov Garden was designed by architect Yaakov Rechter who also designed the Charles Bronfman Auditorium. Both mark the heydays of late Modernism in Israel, also called Brutalism. As part of the general renovation of the square in 2010, the ramp leading from Chen Boulevard toward the square was lowered, and a continuous passage between Habima Square and the boulevards was created. The garden is built on two levels, stairs to the side of the Charles Bronfman Auditorium lead to the sycamore trees.

Yael Schmidt

Yael Schmidt

Charles Bronfman Auditorium

027 B

2 Huberman Street
[A] Dov Karmi, Zeev Rechter, Yaakov Rechter
[R] Kolker, Kolker, Epstein
1957, 2013

The Charles Bronfman Auditorium (Heichal HaTarbut) is the largest concert hall in Tel Aviv and home of the Israel Philharmonic Orchestra. It was planned by leading architects of Modernism and marks the turning point to Brutalism. At the time of construction, the building's novelty lay in its exposed construction and the way it opens up toward the adjacent square. In 2013, the building was renovated in order to serve the contemporary needs of the Philharmonic Orchestra. The main goal was to improve its acoustics, which was undertaken by one of the world's top acoustics engineers, Yesuhisa Toyota, who, amongst other projects, also planned the acoustics of the Elbphilharmonie in Hamburg, Germany. The ceiling was reconstructed, and equipped with perforated, reflective aluminium panels in order to better distribute the sound throughout the hall. In addition, a second 400-seat multipurpose hall was installed underground to be used as a rehearsal hall. The main 2,500-seat main hall was renovated, and the entire building was reinforced against earthquakes. Since it might look as if the auditorium had not significantly changed after the elaborate renovation work, some critics where raising the question how the amount of 140 million shekel was spent. Ironically, the quality of good preservation measures shows if a building looks more or less the same after renovation.

Courtesy by Kolker, Kolker, Epstein

Philipp Meuser

iStock (chameleonseye)

027 B

Alexander Farnsworth

Habima National Theatre **028 B**

2 Tarsat Boulevard
[A] Oskar Kaufmann, Eugen Stolzer
[R] Ram Karmi
1935, 2007

Habima National Theatre is the first public building on Tel Aviv's cultural forum, built according to Geddes' Garden City plan that had envisioned a cultural acropolis at this location. Designed by Oskar Kaufmann, the famous German theatre architect of the 1920s, Habima National Theatre is considered to be the most important of his projects in Israel. It became the largest theatre in the Middle East of that period. Kaufmann left the country before the end of the construction, and his partner Eugen Stolzer completed the project. The rounded, south-facing façade is supported by six round columns, behind which is the stage tower of the main hall. The structure is devoid of decoration, although in the initial design there were theatrical figures included on the western façade. The building was drastically renovated three times, altering its appearance completely. During the last renovation in 2017, the main colonnade was closed with large glass vitrines and the main entrance changed. The arrangement of the halls was altered, as well, and the roof structure was raised for better acoustics. Although the building changed over the years, one can still see the similarity between the Berliner Volksbühne (also designed by Kaufmann) and the Habima Theatre in Tel Aviv. Mainly in the general distribution of the building volume and the rounded front with its six support columns. The original hall itself, which followed the winding façade, the arrangement of the stage and the back rooms were identical to the design of the Volksbühne in Berlin.

Jewish National Fund

Theatre upon completion, 1935

Landesarchiv Berlin

Volksbühne in Berlin, around 1950

Philipp Meuser

Philipp Meuser

The sculpture *Uprise* (Menashe Kadishman, 1967–1976) symbolises the unstable economy and high inflation rate in Israel during this time.

House Ariav

029 B

9 Tarsat Boulevard
[A] Genia Averbuch, Shlomo Ginzburg
[R] Nitza Szmuk Architects
1933, 2017

Ariav House is situated on an elevated platform, two metres above street level, overlooking Habima Square. This building is composed of two building volumes, with the main volume being oriented towards the east toward Tarsat Boulevard. A more modest volume is oriented toward the west, facing Hissin Street, from which it is set back by four metres. The proportions are composed of golden ratio rectangles and almost perfect squares. The eastern building volume has the shape of a cube and lies on top of the ground floor. This creates a slight height difference between the two volumes, granting a clear yet subtle segmentation of the masses. The volumes intersect at the main stairway, which features a thermometer window to regulate the temperature inside the building and to emphasise the play of light and shadow. The eastern façade is distinguished by a row of drawer-like balconies. The balconies are composed of a frontal concrete parapet, which is connected to the façade by four iron bars. This not only allows ventilation but also expresses the different possibilities of using concrete and steel. The building was refurbished in 2017 and a stepped-back rooftop floor was added which is almost unseen from the street level. This project shows how new elements were added to the original building in order to meet current building regulations. One example is the glass cladding behind the balconies' iron bars.

Philipp Meuser

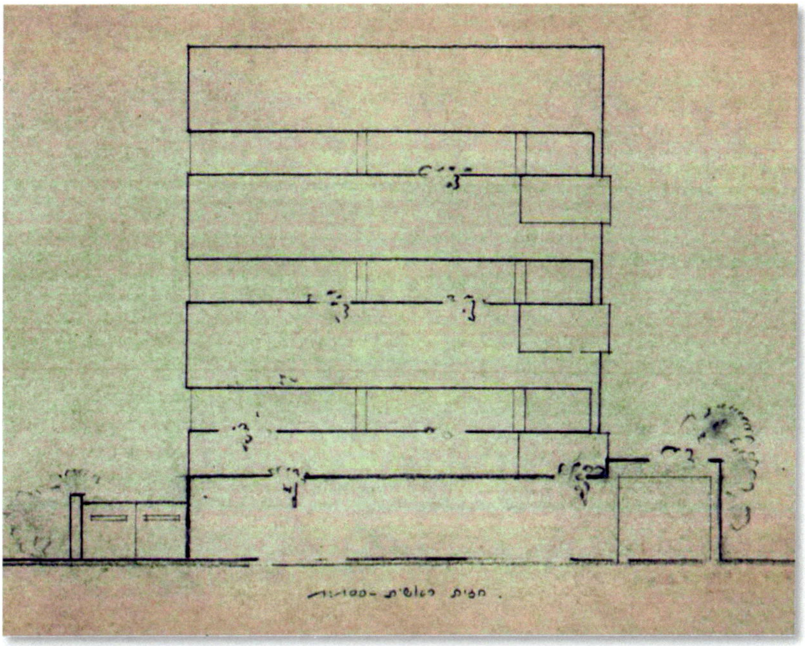

Municipal Archive

Philipp Meuser

House Jacobson 030 B

1 Tarsat Boulevard
[A] Josef Minor
1936

This residential building is situated parallel to the edge of the Habima Cultural Forum. Its front façade is meticulously designed to offer a broad view across the square. The building's main façades intersect at a curved shape, which lends the building volume a fluid appearance and signifies its location on the edge of the cultural compound. It is elevated on a platform to compensate for the height difference to the steep Ben Zion Boulevard and thus features a wide and distinctive main entrance. Horizontality is accentuated by elongated balconies on the building's main façades. The balconies feature bulging handrails that create long narrow shades. The building's staircase is located in tangency to the entrance stairway facing Ben Zion Boulevard. The original design proposed the staircase to feature a thermometer window, but eventually Josef Minor decided to incorporate wide and narrow windows, to further accentuate horizontality. The verticality of the staircase is emphasised by a protruding frame. Throughout the years, the building went through many changes and alterations. A storey was added on the roof, balconies were closed, and windows were modified. Currently, a new refurbishment measure is planned in which most of the additions will be removed. It is worthwhile to check out the staircase railing inside the building.

Itzhak Kalter

Denis Esakov

Itzhak Kalter

Itzhak Kalter

House Efroni

031 B

95 Ahad Ha'am Street
[A] Shlomo Bernstein
1937

This house was built as an alteration to an existing one-storey modernist villa, that was designed by architect Shlomo Gepstein in the year 1931. The new building was designed by architect Shlomo Bernstein who was born in Vilna and immigrated to Palestine in 1924. After studying architecture at the Technion in Haifa, Bernstein decided to extend his studies at the Bauhaus School in Dessau, at the time managed by Ludwig Mies van der Rohe. After graduating from Bauhaus, Bernstein worked briefly in Le Corbusier's atelier in Paris before returning to Palestine. The renovation of House Efroni included adding two additional storeys, turning it into a five-apartment building with a commercial space on the ground floor facing the street corner. The building's façade is asymmetrical and is separated by the vertical glass wall of the staircase. The glazing slightly protrudes from the façade, after installation it was completely transparent since the architect aimed to create a coherent connection between the semi-private staircase and the public street. The roof terrace testifies to the fact that the upper roof area was used for daily life. The balconies' balustrades feature a detail unique to this building. Instead of designing a standard flat surface balustrade commonly made of silicate bricks and plaster, this balustrade is made of perforated concrete to allow optimal ventilation. The pattern might be influenced by the *Mashrabia*, an element common to Arab vernacular building tradition that is used for ventilation.

House Fried

032 B

91-93 Ahad Ha'am Street
[A] Zeev Rechter
1937

Designed by one of Tel Aviv's leading architects of the 1930s, House Fried was built on an extremely narrow plot that borders three streets; thus, it has the peculiar shape of a high, narrow box. Across three storeys, it comprises five apartments and a commercial space on the ground floor. The plot's irregular, long and narrow shape in conjunction with urban regulations that require a certain setback from the parcel's borders dictated the building's narrow southern part with the façade being only four metres wide. Here, Rechter designed three consecutive rooms parallel to a long, far protruding balcony. This balcony can also serve as an exterior corridor, merging the boundaries between the interior and the exterior. Moreover, its oversized wireframe balustrade enhances the connection between the street and the apartment. The narrow shape of the floorplan and the lack of interior corridors allow the apartment to be cross ventilated regularly. Originally, the building featured a wide entrance with glass doors, which were removed

Itzhak Kalter

at the time of World War II, when Italy, which in 1940 declared war on Britain, attacked Palestine from the air, which was ruled by a British Mandate Power at the time. In addition, a wall was constructed to partly block the entrance, serving as shelter in case of air bombings.

Perhaps one should consider leaving the temporary wall when renovating as part of the building's history. Rechter probably would never have imagined that his choice to recess the building form the plot's sharp angle would suit so perfectly for a coffee shop, as it is used today.

Municipal Arcive

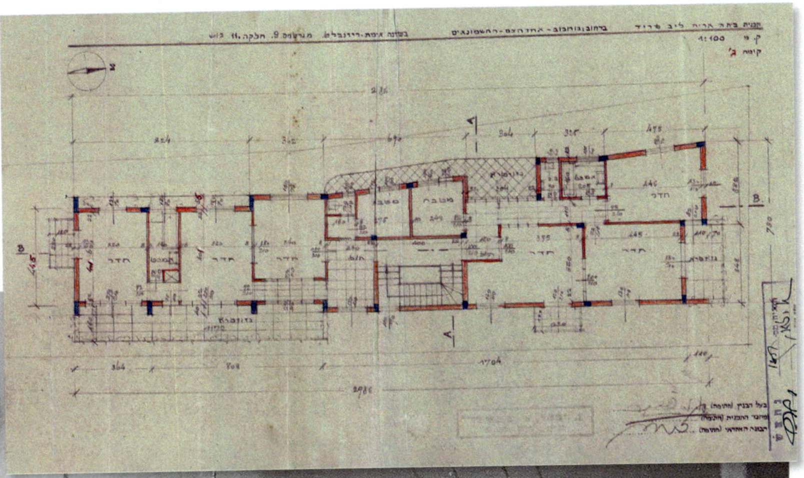

House Aharonovich

033 B

117 Rothschild Boulevard
[A] Yitzchak Rapoport
[R] Amnon Bar Or – Tal Gazit Architects
1933

This extraordinary house is located on a slight slope named "The Rider's Hill" after the ranch that used to stand on this spot. It was built as a part of the planned expansion to the Rothschild Avenue towards the north. With its three storeys, the dimensions of this residential building resemble those of most of the other buildings in the area. House Aharonovich is composed of three rectangular volumes offset from one another. The resulting expansive building envelope facilitates cross-ventilation of the individual rooms. The space created between each pair of overlapping volumes contains a stairway with a rounded thermometer window. The three building volumes contain six apartments each. Every zone has its own entrance, one facing Rothschild Avenue and the other facing Bar-Ilan Street. The building's edge is softened by a rounded corner, emphasizing the novelty and virtuosity of construction possibilities enabled by the International Style. The garden is an integral part of the building design, which, after its renovation in 2018, also received an underground parking garage. Due to its extraordinary features, the House Aharonovich was listed as a monument subject to strict preservation regulations (one out of 190). Therefore, the building permit to expand the top storey was sold to a project that was subject to less stringent regulations.

Itzhak Kalter

Philipp Meuser

Kurt Bremer

House Sarah Rapoport

034 B

118 Rothschild Boulevard
[A] Yitzchak Rapoport
[R] Rapoport Architects
1932-1934

House Sarah Rapoport underwent many construction phases. Originally built in 1932 as a one-storey residential villa, two more storeys were added during the next two years. Originally the facade was designed to emphasize the corner, as the next plot to the north was used as a garden and pool by the residents of the villa. The main façade is divided into three vertical planes, of which the centre plane is set as an anchor point featuring the building's extravagant entrance staircase windows. The entrance is marked by a wide concrete shading cornice that is repeated in a smaller fashion as a shading element above the horizontal staircase window – the thermometer window. The northern façade features a set of "flying balconies". They are built with concrete slab floors and metal pipe banisters that grant them a feeling of lightness, reflecting the new construction capabilities of the modern movement that uses slender slabs of steel and concrete. The concrete roof pergola was destroyed along the years but still serves as a framing element marking the top contour of the building. In 2010, two additional storeys were added. Only one storey with horizontal windows was added to the front building volume, which means that the different construction phases can be easily distinguished. The larger building volume at the rear of the building is three storeys higher than the front volume. The new block was rendered with a smooth plaster finish in order to distinguish it from the existing building parts, creating a passe-partout-like frame and honouring the plasticity of the original building. Although the addition changes the buildings proportions significantly and doubled the residential units, the original façade was carefully preserved to its former glory.

Yael Schmidt

Philipp Meuser

House Mossinson 035 B

14 Ha'Gilboa Street

[A] Pinchas Bijonski

[R] Bar Orian Architects-Tal Gazit Architects

1933

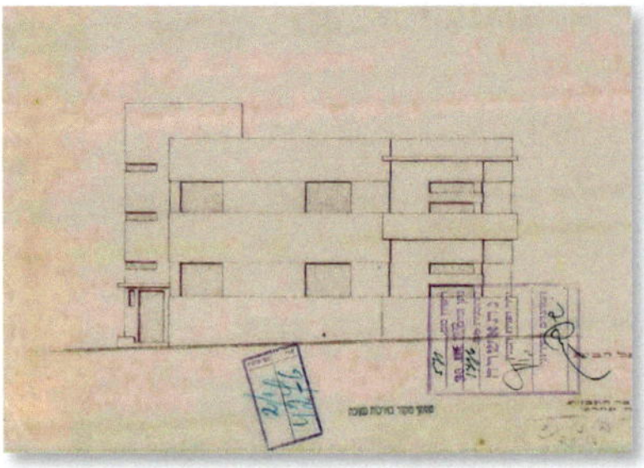

Municipal Archive

This town villa was a rare typology at the time of its construction, demonstrating the lifestyle of the elite. The villa was commissioned by Dr. Ben-Tzion Mossinson, who was one of Tel Aviv's first landowners and the first principle of the Herzliya Hebrew Gymnasium – the school building which was one of Tel Aviv's historic landmarks. The house was his family home, accommodating him and his wife on the upper floor, and his daughter's family on the lower floor. The building stands out not only for its relatively small dimensions but also for its recess from the street, which allowed for a spacious garden. The building's composition is asymmetrical, its façades are free of ornamentation. The apertures and balconies are designed according to the building's westward orientation. The space between the windows is made of fair-faced silicate bricks to emphasize the building's horizontality and the construction materials of the time. Over the years, the building was expanded on its eastern side, while the front façade kept its original form. It is currently undergoing renovation, including the addition of another, recessed storey on the roof.

Philipp Meuser

Permanently installed boardgame in a city park on Ha'Gilboa Street

Philipp Meuser

House Rubinsky

036 B

65 Shenkin Street
[A] Lucian Korngold
[A] Bar Orian Architects, Amnon Bar Or - Tal Gazit Architects
1935

House Rubinsky clearly demonstrates the "Five points toward a new architecture" that Le Corbusier demanded. 1: *Piloti* ('columns') – the *piloti* were used to create a shaded garden that was open toward the incoming sea breeze. 2: The liberated façade – demonstrated by the corner of the building, which seems slightly disconnected from the main building volume. 3: Ribbon windows – their arrangement emphasises the building's horizontal orientation. 4: The flat roof with garden – an element typical for all modernistic buildings in the city. 5: The free floorplan – the building is constructed with a frame made of reinforced concrete (instead of the load-bearing walls typical of earlier constructions), enabling much greater flexibility in the arrangement of the rooms. Each of the three building volumes that make up the overall building contains one apartment per storey. As is customary for International Style buildings, House Rubinsky lacks any ornamentation but, in a way, this principle is reversed by an excessive use of drainage openings along the balconies. Most of them are designed for purely ornamental reasons with only a few actually serving as drainage. The building design is inspired by the great ocean liners, the icons of the machine age, that influenced even Le Corbusier's designs. Exemplary details include the round bull-eye windows and the steel piping used as railing elements. Since each façade of the building looks different, it is recommended to walk around the building and look at it from all sides. Although House Rubinsky was designed by architect Lucian Korngold, he never signed the building plan. Instead, two of his colleagues did, both of whom where later murdered in Auschwitz. Korngold himself emigrated to San Paulo, Brazil.

Denis Esakov

Michal Bar Or

Denis Esakov

Irmel Kamp-Bandau

House Buksenbaum

037 B

6 Bilu Street

Arieh Striemer

1937

The round balconies and the fluid form of the rounded building corners are influenced by the streamline modernism of German Jewish Architect Erich Mendelsohn. The building's sculptural nothern façade features long, rounded, and slightly recessed balconies. This is contrasted by the rectangular mass of the building volume on the south side. The balconies on the façade facing west have ventilation slots to allow wind flow and cooling. The bulging, round balconies resembling Mendelsohn's style are extremely delicately crafted. The thin profile of the concrete balconies and their continuous slots demonstrate the excellent craftsmanship of the builders at the time and their understanding of the then new material.

Denis Esakov

Denis Esakov

House Handel Pelman 038 B

Engel Sreet 8
[A] Y. Schwartz and A. Hirsch
[R] Plesner Architects
1936

This three-storey, L-shaped building has a small front garden that functions as a semi-public buffer zone at the building's entrance, fulfilling the vision of Geddes' plan for Tel Aviv as a Garden City. The building is composed of two building volumes that generate an expansive building envelope which allows for cross-ventilation, as each room points at at least two cardinal directions. The two horizontal building volumes intersect at the vertical stairway, which is signified by a thermometer window. The steel frames of the windows resemble the aesthetics of Art Deco. The western part of the façade features extremely recessed concrete balconies with an apron that provide a shading effect as the upper balcony shades the one below it. The rear building volume is recessed from the parcel's boundaries, and it is half a storey higher than the front volume. The curved balconies on this part of the façade represent the ship motif of the International Style, influenced here by German architect Erich Mendelsohn and his Streamline Modernism. Taking a closer look at the detailing shows the virtuosity of how the builders worked with concrete: the curved lines of the balconies seem virtually glued to the façade. Try to also take a look inside the building since the ornamented steel railing of the stairway is certainly worth a visit. The building was renovated in 2018, whereby its original shape was maintained.

Philipp Meuser

Philipp Meuser

Philipp Meuser

House Aginski
5 Engel Street
[A] Sam Barkay
1934

039 B

Architect Sam Barkay left Palestine to study architecture in Venice and Paris, and worked as an apprentice in Le Corbusier's atelier, which deeply influenced his work. The main façade of this building faces south and small window openings and ribbons of recessed balconies coin the front of the building. The staircase's south wing incorporates a curtain wall façade made of square glass tiles that resemble Pierre Chareau's 1931 Glass House in Paris. It is the only building of the kind left in Tel Aviv. It can be assumed that Barkay was influenced by Le Corbusier's use of glass tiles in his early designs, and most prominently by the iconic Maison de Verre, one of the first modernist buildings with a glass tile curtain wall. Barkay understood that glass walls contribute to heating the spaces they confine, and therefore designed apertures to allow ventilation of the stairway. The façade comprises a vertical formation of three French balconies, which softens the distance between the recessed balcony ribbons on either side. It is possible that the balconies were influenced by the iconic balconies of the Bauhaus student ward in Dessau, Germany, by famed architect Walter Gropius.

Philipp Meuser

Itzhak Kalter

Itzhak Kalter

House Cytak-Zeitig and House Yitzchaki

040 B

89-91 Rothschild Boulevard

[A] Pinchas (Philip) Hütt

1935

These two buildings were built and designed together and represent the "twin house" typology. Each of these buildings, built on a double lot, is a mirror reflection of the other. The layout of the two L-shaped buildings forms a large garden, that creates an intermediate area between the street and the building, interrupts the urban mass and expands the street area. At the time of construction, Rothschild Boulevard was the only green artery in Tel Aviv. Each building is three storeys high and contains two four-room apartments on each floor. The buildings are located on the north-south oriented part of Rothschild Boulevard, thus creating a situation in which the southern building shades the garden during the daytime. The entrances are located at the intersection of the two building volumes, thus obliging the residents to enter through the garden. Bulging balconies embellish the façades and prevent solar radiation from reaching the apartments through the openings, while also enhancing the horizontal aspect of the buildings. The balconies' round and narrow section protrudes the front façade and features a concrete skirt extruding from its lower part. Although the buildings share the same shape, they differ in the way that the shape reflects the play of light and shadow. In order to fully understand the intention of the architect one has to imagine the building in its original state in which both the protruding, round balconies as well as the recessed balconies were open.

Philipp Meuser

Philipp Meuser

House Baumöl 041 B
87 Rothschild Boulevard
[A] Carl Rubin
1936

The building was designed by architect Carl Rubin who also designed the adjacent building to the south on 85 Rothschild Boulevard four years prior. Both buildings share the same basic concept of an L-shaped floorplan. During the 1930s, Tel Aviv's population was overflowing with immigrants, in need of fast housing. Like many other buildings at the time this three-storey building was erected replacing a one-storey building built on the plot before. The building is composed of two intersecting rectangular volumes, one of which is recessed towards the back of the plot to create a semi-public space. The ground floor features a garage and a garden functioning as its driveway. The building's main façade is oriented eastward, a setting which prevents direct ventilation by means of the sea breeze. In order to overcome the ventilation challenge, Rubin designed the apartments with openings to the west in a manner that every room features at least two openings facing different directions for cross ventilation. The front façade's horizontal emphasis is achieved by incorporating long, recessed balconies facing two different directions. The northern part of the front balcony features a unique glass wall, blurring the border between the inside and the outside. Archival documents show that Rubin was not granted permission to complete this glass detail, although it was eventually built as intended. The large variety of balconies in Tel Aviv, in general, has created a vivid social interaction between the residents and the street. Take a look at the narrow steel milk elevator placed on the building's northern façade.

Itzhak Kalter

Philipp Meuser

House Dr. Sadovsky

042 B

85 Rothschild Boulevard
[A] Carl Rubin
[R] Bar Orian Architects
1933

The building was designed by Carl Rubin, the same architect who also designed the adjacent building to the north. Constructed as a split, L-shaped cube with a front garden the design improves the breeze circulating through the building. The architect emphasised the horizontality common to the International Style buildings of the time by means of recessed balconies and wide windows. Here, the effect was underlined with bulging balconies expanding across the eastern façade. Three additional storeys were added to the building in 2014. During construction, the house was raised to allow for an underground parking level. Looking closely, one can clearly spot the building addition as the thermometer window stretches only across the building's original height. The first added storey follows the original floorplan using the same building materials, while the top two storeys are recessed and constructed with different materials. This building shows the challenging task that preservation poses: additional storeys need to be added while keeping the horizontal emphasis and proportions of the original structure.

Philipp Meuser

Philipp Meuser

House Engel

043 B

84 Rothschild Boulevard
[A] Zeev Rechter
[R] Bar Orian Architects,
Amnon Bar Or - Tal Gazit Architects
1933

"It does not get more Corbusier then this in Tel Aviv" states the architect responsible for the restoration in an interview: this building is one of the architectural milestones in the development of residential buildings in the first Hebrew city. The house started as an idea by Sarah Engel, a Jewish entrepreneur who immigrated from England asking to build a quality rental apartment. Like today, there was a high demand for rental housing at the time, yielded very handsome income to entrepreneurs. Rechter, a young architect just returning from his studies, turned to be one of the most prominent architects of the time. He designed exclusively according to the modernist principles of Le Corbusier, the father of modernist architecture, incorporating, pilotis, flat roof gardens and ribbon windows, whereby their size was reduced to accommodate for the great heat that prevails in the country. In addition, a concrete frame was implemented to shade them from the strong sunlight. With his use of *pilotis*, Rechter has strongly influenced the appearance of the White City, as the majority of buildings built in the second half of the 1930s where imitating this principle. The U-shape of the Engel House is composed of straight angles, it is asymmetrical, and is matched to the lines of the plot and the street. In combination with the *piloti* floor, this enhances the flow of air from the sea to the apartments. It also created a semi-public, semi-private space that connects the street to the privacy of the apartment, a meeting point and a place for social interaction between the families who live in the building. This building is one of the city's 190 listed building under strict conservation law which may not receive any additional storeys. Instead, it is possible to sell the building rights to another building. However, after its 4-year-long renovation, the conservation department has granted an addition of two living units on the roof, in what used to be the former work-out room. The reasons for the relatively long renovation time was the construction of machine rooms and a large, fully automated parking system, which can hold up to 26 cars underground. Entrance and exit from the car park are possible through the inner courtyard. As the courtyard is also listed for conservation, the parking lot is invisible unless it is being opened.

Itzhak Kalter

Itzhak Kalter

Itzhak Kalter

House Rubinsky-Braun

044 B

82 Rothschild Boulevard
[A] Zeev and Joseph Berlin
[R] Bar-Orian Architects
1932

House Rubinsky-Braun demonstrates the stylistic shift of the early 1930s in Tel Aviv, from decorative and ornament-oriented styles such as Art Deco and Eclecticism to the functionality-driven International Style. The corner lot building is composed of two symmetrical building volumes that are connected by a stairway and whose façades curve toward the central staircase. The staircase's thermometer window is composed of an angular glass curtain wall that protrudes vertically above the building's top banister. The flat top of the window is offset outward to reference the plane motif used by modernist architect Le Corbusier in his book 'Toward an Architecture'. The two building volumes adjoining the staircase feature a strong horizontal emphasis achieved by a careful arrangement of recessed and protruding balconies, wide windows, and a special surface finish of the ribbon window that slope toward the staircase. Whereas the International Style aims at abolishing symmetry in architecture, this building uses its strictly symmetrical shape and its irregular lot shape to serve as the focal point for its location. As the building is subject to the strict preservation regulations, a so-called invisible extension was added, which is recessed from

the front façade and houses a rooftop apartment. A concrete core with shelter rooms that reinforces the building against earthquakes was integrated on the building's rear side. A set of large, slidable wooden shading elements were mounted on this installation to soften its harsh concrete appearance. Please take a look at the entrance to the staircase and spot the borderline between the original Terrazzo floor and the newly designed, landscaped garden.

Municipal Archive

Denis Esakov

Yzchak Marglit House

045 B

69 Rothschild Boulevard
[A] Yzchak Schwartz
[R] AN+
1932

This building exemplifies typical attributes of the International Style: an asymmetrical façade, split building volumes allowing greater air circulation, emphasised horizontality, and a vertical thermometer window. In 1933, another storey was added designed by the same architect. In 2019, the building underwent renovation including the addition of three additional storeys which were joined together to be turned into apartment hotel, planned by the two young and upcoming architects Avital Gourary and Natanel Elfassy. The addition comprises spaces of different height, some designed as terraced gardens with varied vegetation. The aim was to create a floating garden above the trees of the avenue, dissolving the boundaries between the exterior and the interior by the means of a transparent structure. In redefining the traditional relationship between building and ground, the sectional quality of the design is not a horizontal distribution of the spaces but rather a multi-level programme, providing rooms with distinctly different characteristics and views.

Aviad Bar Ness

Philipp Meuser

3D Visualization: Jonathan Kleinhample

Naparstag Heuschreck House

046 B

48 Rothschild Boulevard
[A] Pinchas (Philip) Hütt
[R] AN+
1934

The building stands on a platform and highlights the typical attributes of the International Style. Its long and rounded balconies that protrude beyond the building volume refer to the reinforced concrete construction method. The balconies also form small aprons that shade the balconies beneath them. Originally, the façade featured delicate plaster work that enhanced the building's verticality. The front windows feature typical wooden shutters whereas the back façade has traditional Arab shutters. The next renovation plan envisions to connect the historical building with a new, transparent building volume, which will visually connect the boulevard with the garden on the rear side of the house. Creating a passage between 48 Rothschild, 46 Rothschild (HESEG House), and Elrov Tower; thus, opening the future hotel toward the city. The entrances are accessible from all directions. Generous public spaces and a brasserie will occupy the new ground floor on the street level. The attraction will not only be the hotel but the building itself: raised and thus visually separated from the ground, it will draw visitors inside.

3D Visualization: Lőrincz Áron, Photography: Aviad Bar Ness

Meier on Rothschild 047 B
36 Rothschild Boulevard
[A] Richard Meier
2007-2016

This residential high-rise was designed by Pritzker Award-winning architect Richard Meier. The building is composed of 42 storeys, although the initial building permit allowed only 32 storeys. The additional ten storeys were achieved by transferring building rights as part of the urban conservation plan that allows such transfers in specific cases (see introduction on The UNESCO declaration to learn more). In this case, the building right was transferred from the strictly protected House Romanov (mentioned in tour 3). The high-rise design was inspired by the principles of the International Style, which can be seen in the emphasis on functionality, the use of modern industrially produced materials, and the repetitive modules. Even though the white façade cladding pays tribute to the local International Style, the climatic solutions used here refer to late modernism (Brutalism), in which it was common to use brise-soleil sun protection elements. The vertical shelter rooms were stationed in the centre of the tower to avoid sealed concrete walls in the façade. The same is true for the structural columns, which were placed inside the apartments to allow for a free, transparent façade. The building includes luxurious enmities including a gym, a wine cellar, a spacious lobby, and a 25-metre-long swimming pool that is located above the renovated passage. The tower complies with the U.S. Green Standard Certificate and contributes to energy savings by using special shading elements and an air conditioning system for irrigation of the vegetation. In addition, each storey is equipped with separate recycling funnels for glass, paper and plastic. Despite its location on the less attractive side of Rothschild Boulevard – here, the boulevard crosses the somewhat run-down Allenby Street – a penthouse is typically offered for 170 million Israeli shekel (roughly 42.5 million Euro).

Philipp Meuser

Philipp Meuser

Minzer House

048 B

18 Rothschild Boulevard
[A] Pinchas (Philip) Hütt
[R] Amnon Bar Or
1934, 2015

This monument-listed building on 18 Rothschild Boulevard represent some of the typical qualities of the movement of the International Style. It was built in a period of rapid development, historical Tel Aviv changed from a residential neighbourhood to a vivid metropolis. The main element characterising this building is the horizontal emphasis provided by the window ribbons, which run around the entire building. The repetitive use of the same window formats reveals its original use as an office building. The concrete cornice that surrounds the building above the ground floor emphasises the clear separation between the entrance lobby and the office floors above. One year after completion of the building, entrepreneur Avraham Yosef Minzer bought the next vacant plot on 20 Rothschild Boulevard, and had another house built by the same architect. The renovation project in 2015 merged together the two buildings. The resulting ensemble is used for Edmond de Rothschild Bank's activities in Israel. The rear building part of 18 Rothschild was renovated to include two additional storeys. In order to enable a functional unity of the two buildings, a new glass wing was designed that connects the existing buildings. This glass wing is offset to the rear of the lot, which makes the two buildings appear as two separate entities when viewed from the front although they are factually connected. The main entrance lobby is situated in the original location of the historic lobby but was refurbished and completely newly designed. Please also take a look at the Founders' Memorial including a fountain in front of the building. It remembers the 66 families that cast lots to found what is now Tel Aviv.

Municipal Archive

Denis Esakov

Philipp Meuser

Amnon Bar Or Architects

Philipp Meuser

Memorial for the founders of Tel Aviv (Artist: Aaron Priver, 1949)

IT Studio

16 Rothschild Boulevard

049 B

[A] Carl Rubin
[R] Uri Glazer,
Nili Gal Master Architects
1934

This building was the residence of the first mayor of Tel Aviv, Meir Dizengoff. Originally, it was built as a one-storey-building as was typical for the neighbourhood around 1910. When, in 1930, Dizengoff's wife died, the mayor decided to donate his home in her memory to serve as a museum. In 1934, the building was remodelled from an Eclectic Style residence to a modernist public building by architect Carl Rubin who was a student of Erich Mendelsohn: it became the new Tel Aviv Museum of Art and Culture. On May14, 1948, David Ben-Gurion declared the establishment of the State of Israel in this very house as part of a short, 40-minute-long ceremony. The place was chosen as the most suitable to host the People's Council for the festive ceremony, in part because it was considered relatively safe from possible bombardments by the air forces of the Arab countries due to its small window openings and its reinforced concrete structure. The hall on the first floor was quickly set up for the announcement, with the nearby cafés providing chairs for the venue. Ben-Gurion read the declaration of independence to 350 guests, while the crowd outside was able to listen via loudspeakers. The building is currently being refurbished, and the exhibition is enlarged. The renovation will restore the ground floor back to the *Zeitgeist* of 1948, except for small deviations such as the exposure of a window from Dizengoff's original home in the western part of the house, as a glance to the more distant past. In addition, a ceramic relief depicting a menorah and olive leaves was discovered on the ground floor, hitherto hidden and unknown.

Israel Ministry of Foreign Affairs/Rudi Weissenstein

B

Philipp Meuser

Eliavazon House 050 B

7 Rothschild Boulevard
[A] Yosef Kashdan
[R] Amnnon Bar Or Tal Gazit architects 2005
1934

The original building was built in 1909 as part of the first settlement of Tel Aviv, carrying the name Achuzat Bayit. Most of the original building was destroyed in the 1930s, and this modernistic building was built instead. The new structure was designed in an L-shape, the main façade shows the architectural language typical to the modern style, including horizontally framed windows topped by vertical cornices, and cantilevered balconies. Emphasis on the building's corner was achieved through the curved shape and a geometrical distribution of the volumes. This corresponds to the parallel

Denis Esakov

building on 4 Herzl Street, which was also planned as part of the new front. The renovation measures comprised the building envelope and the stairwell, and included adding a new wing on the western açade facing the new square. Following the renovation, the building's ground floor was converted into office and commercial spaces. It was purchased by the French government and currently serves as a centre for French culture.

Itzhak Kalter

Model Houses of Modernity

Dizengoff Square, 1934

Library of Congress

Philipp Meuser

Dizengoff Square and its Surroundings

This tour features the best example of the UNESCO world cultural heritage White City – both in terms of the original Garden City Plan by Patrick Geddes and the best practice character of the buildings.

The area was established in the second half of the 1930s, hence many of its buildings were constructed in the International Style, which was already prescribed by city regulations.

Most of the buildings feature a horizontal emphasis, and are built on *piloti*, those columns that Le Corbusier propagates in his 'Five points towards a new architecture'. They not only allow for lush gardenscapes beneath the buildings but provide a ventilation effect, as well, both of which were part of the "total design" of these buildings. The gardens created a microclimate and a pleasant entry situation to the buildings, acting as a buffer zone between the public street and the private space.

The carefully designed gardens, the lobbies that often included benches and small fish ponds; these entrances along with the planned hierarchy between the streets and the sizes of the plots, and last but not least the relationship between building height and street width all express the Garden City principles according to Geddes. An example of the typical Geddes block can be experienced toward the end of this tour at the Ruth garden.

Dizengoff square, the starting point of this tour, was planned to serve as a public

Dizengoff Square, 2019

plaza, as already as in the first and original plan for Tel Aviv by Patrick Geddes. The building permit for the tall, white tower north of the square was granted before the UNESCO declaration in 2003. Hence, it marks an exception as the declared UNESCO zone forbids buildings in excess of six storeys in dense areas such as Dizengoff Street.

Another highlight of the International Style in Tel Aviv is the co-operative housing ensemble Hod which embodies not only the aesthetic attributes but also the social aspects of modernism in the country. Designed by Bauhaus architect Arieh Sharon in 1933, it expresses the pioneering approach of the General Organisation of Workers Histadrut to establish a new urban lifestyle, in the spirit of socialism and – particularly in the case of this building – in correlation with the teachings of the second Bauhaus principal Hannes Meyer, who influenced architect Arieh Sharon's in his work.

1935

Library of Congress, G. Eric and Edith Matson Photograph Collection (Courtesy of the Israel Museum)

Zina Dizengoff Square

051 C

1-16 Zina Dizengoff Square
[A] Genia Averbuch
1935 -1957

The beating heart of Tel Aviv was designed by the city's first lady of Modernism, Genia Averbuch. In many European countries, the Avantgarde of Modernism had become the *lingua franca*, although the style was still confronted with old traditions in which female architects were not considered part of the inner circles. Thanks to its first principle Walter Gropius, the Bauhaus Dessau was praised for its progressiveness by accepting women to study architecture while, before, this had been impossible.

Genia Averbuch was only 20 years old when, in 1934, she won the first prize of a competition for the design of Dizengoff Square. Apparently, only a few years before, a very similar entry had won first prize for a competition for the design of Alexanderplatz in Berlin, which is likely to had immediate influence on her plan for Dizengoff Square. During the 1920s, Alexanderplatz was a Berlin icon and a junction of department stores and mobility. At the time, leading architecture firms were invited to participate a design competition for the square, among them pioneers of the modern style such as Mies van der Rohe. The prestigious judging committee, whose members included architect Erich Mendelsohn, choose the design of the brothers Vasily and Hans Lockhart and Alphonse Anker which, however, was never realised. The main motif of their plans for Alexanderplatz was a clear horizontal structure, designed to create uniformity in the square. The dynamic flow of the lines forming a whole circle was a tribute to the constant coming on going on the square.

These motifs also served as the underlying concept for the design of Dizengoff Square. However, in Tel Aviv, the buildings received an additional layer in the shape of long and narrow balconies covering the

entire front façades and functioning as a climate regulator for the buildings' interior. The balconies and protruding building elements protect the inner space from the blazing sun, simultaneously creating a modern, three-dimensional look that demonstrated the potential of the new building material concrete, which was the *dernier cri* of the time anyways. The buildings on the square were planned by various architects. Averbuch herself designed only two of these building, in addition to the master plan of the square, of course.

Tel Aviv Municipality

Hotel Cinema (Kolno'a Ester)

052 C

10-12 Dizengoff Square
[A] Yehuda, Rephael Megidovich
[R] Arieh Dwilanski
1938

Since its construction and up until 1998, the building served as a cinema with an auditorium that accommodated 1,000 visitors. It was the second cinema in Tel Aviv owned by a well-established couple who immigrated from Aden, Yemen. This building follows an irregular, semi-trapezoid shape derived from the shape of the plot. Its main façade follows the square's outline as the master plan dictated that all façades should be designed according to the same principle, independent of their function, which in the case of a cinema would not have required balconies. The square's master plan also stipulated that the ground floor of all buildings should be recessed 1.3 metres from the plot boundary. This building's main façade is oriented toward the west which results in strong solar radiation during noon hours. Therefore, the planners decided to recess the ground floor by 3.3 metres to prevent the entry space from heating up and to create a formal entry situation leading to the foyer. Between 1998 and 2001, before Tel Aviv's conservation policy, the building underwent renovation which changed its original function from cinema to hotel. While the renovation included adding elevators, shelter rooms, and two recessed roof floors along with the expansion of the basement, its original form was mainly preserved. Step inside the lobby and take a look at the impressive stairway and the display of original furniture, including items from the former cinema.

Denis Esakov

Denis Esakov

Administration Center Kupat Cholim Clalit

053 C

8 Bellinson Street
[A] Josef Neufeld
1938

This building reflects the architectural principle of "form follows function" as the façade reflects the manifold functions of the building. From the storage facilities in the basement to the reception on the ground floor all the way to the offices above. The Kupat Cholim Clalit was one of only a few public, modernistic buildings in Tel Aviv at the time. Architect Josef Neufeld had studied architecture in Vienna and Rome, he worked in Erich Mendelsohn's office in Berlin and Bruno Taut's office in Moscow. This building served as a storage facility for the private Assuta hospital which issued a competition for the design of its new headquarters building in 1937. Josef Neufeld's design won the competition for its functional approach and the idea of incorporating an existing hole in the plot's centre as a basement for medication storage and laboratories. The large space located on the main floor demonstrates the large free spaces made possible by the use of reinforced concrete. Its convex façade originates from the shape of Dizengoff Square which lies at its rear façade. It allows natural light entering the building. Since the building is oriented toward the west, the design allows exposure to the sea breeze and therefore provides natural ventilation. The building's upper storey, the office storey, and its cubic properties protrude beyond the building volume, hence creating a distinct horizontal emphasis and a play of light and shadow. Today, the building is awaiting renovation permission and is currently serving as a Kabbalah Centre.

Itzhak Kalter

Itzhak Kalter

Philipp Meuser

Philipp Meuser

House Arlozerov - Ohel Theater 054 C

6 Bellinson Street
[A] Arieh Sharon
[R] M. Vered Architects, Amnon Bar-Or Tal Gazit Architects
1939-1940

Built by Israel's national Bauhaus architect Arieh Sharon for the Histadrut – the main workers union in early days Palestine. It housed the collectively run Ohel theatre and a social club for the members of Mapai – the former socialist workers' party. Similar to the neighbouring Kupat Holim Centre, the building follows a convex shape derived from the articulation of Dizengoff square located its back. Despite the fact that the building follows a strict symmetry, it also takes its shape from the different functions it was designed to serve. The front façade features a rectangular mass protruding from it, which distinguishes the main auditorium from the rest of the building. On both sides of the building projected apertures mark the locations of the foyers. Over the years, the building went through noticeable changes, until eventually being abandoned. Today, the building is approved for renovation under strict conservation regulations, to be converted into a boutique hotel.

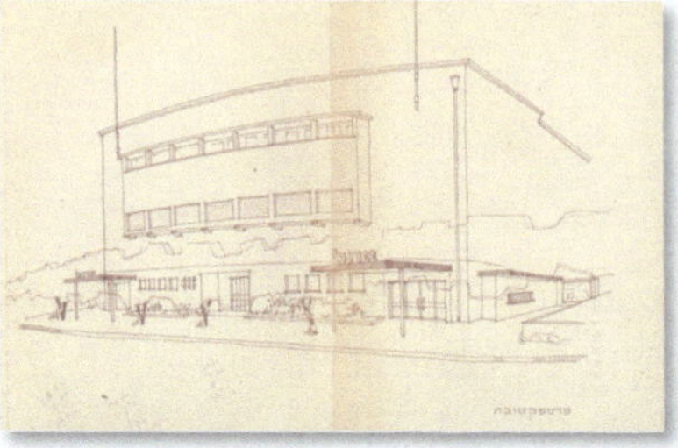

Municipal Archive

Philipp Meuser

Municipal Archive

Denis Esakov

House Hanoch 055 C

10 Aharonovich Street

[A] Barzilay, Houseman

1937

Like many other buildings that were built in the second half of the 1930s, this house features an impressive entrance lobby, lifted on pillars and presenting a wide variety of decorative elements. They include chequerboard pattern tiles, decorative mosaics, meticulously designed handrails, marble wall cladding, and more. The building is divided into two large building volumes as a result of the plot's irregular shape. The main volume is curved and features long balconies that extend across the entire façade, thus emphasising its horizontal orientation. Since the façade does not serve any load-bearing function it was possible to incorporate thin concrete aprons which provide the building with a sense of lightness. In order to further emphasize the horizontality of the building, the balconies feature tubular handrails and protruding elements that create horizontal shadows.

Irmel Kamp-Bandau

Denis Esakov

House Hochzeit II

056 C

13 Aharonovich Street
[A] Shlomo Gepstein
1938

The building is located in the silicate neighbourhood, named after the silicate brick factory which produced the material for the International Style buildings of Tel Aviv. Amongst other applications, the bricks were used as infill for reinforced concrete frame constructions and partition walls. The building is composed of two rectangular volumes of different width. The wider volume features balconies that project outward toward the other volume, making the building seem as if it was composed of one rectangular mass. The International Style objects to the use of decorative elements, thus pushing architects to broaden the boundaries of functional elements. This fact is strongly demonstrated in Gepstein's meticulous design of the balconies, each of which features a protrusion on the lower edge to create a horizontal emphasis with the shadow it casts. In addition, the balconies are equipped with a balustrade composed of concrete and glass sheets, metal framing and tubular handrails. A few years after the building was completed, an apartment was added on the ground floor, which diminished the qualities of the building's original entrance.

Denis Esakov

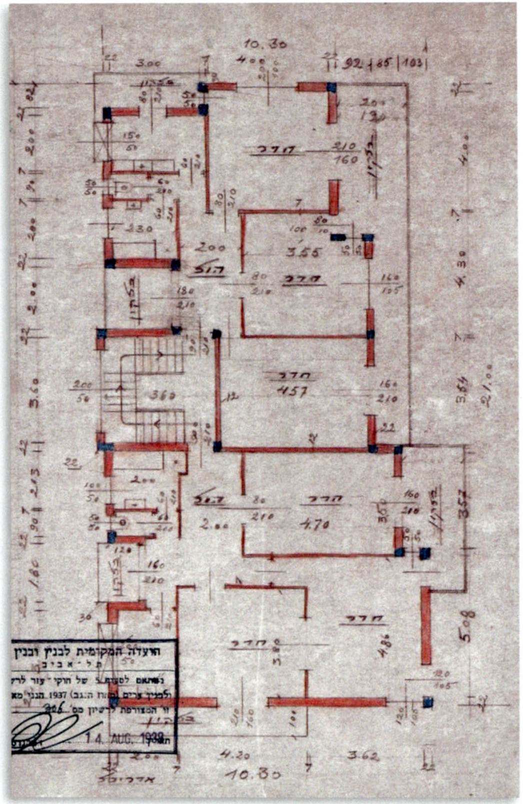

Municipal Archive

Philipp Meuser

House Hochzeit I

057 C

11 Aharonovich Street
[A] Shlomo Gepstein
[R] Gal Peleg Architects
1937

House Hochzeit I was built one year prior to the adjacent building and designed by the same architect, Shlomo Gepstein. The building's floor plan mainly follows a symmetrical axis that is marked by the circulation core's location, around which all service areas are located. The façade emphasises horizontality with long balconies which are framed on one side by the extension of the side wall, which shades the balconies and improves ventilation. Another balcony type is the service balcony on the eastern and western fronts. These balconies are barely visible, since they are part of a niche under the kitchen windows. The main façade facing the street is covered with scratch plaster which also coverers the front parts of the eastern and western facades. The rest of the building is covered with white lime plaster. The entrance features brown ceramic tiles and an impressive set of doors made of wood and glass, the lobby and the stairs include yellow tiles. A renovation of the building in 2014 included adding basement and a recessed storey. The balconies on the rear side where closed with glass and metal frames, and the front garden was replanted.

Philipp Meuser

Municipal Archive

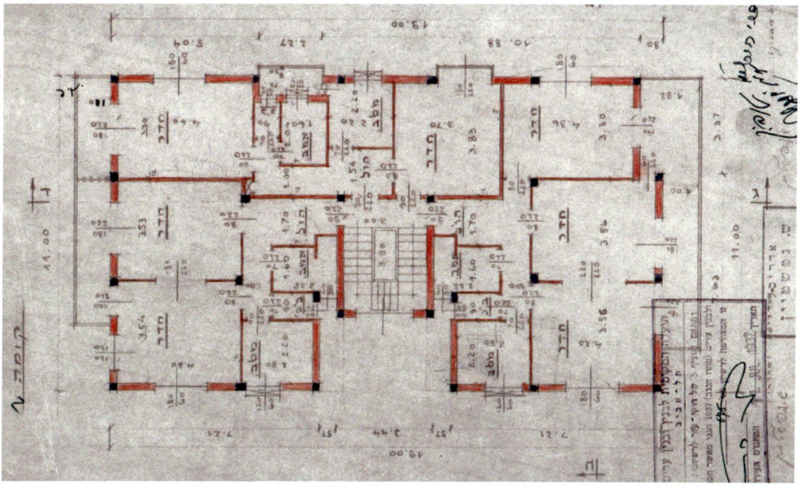

Philipp Meuser

Philipp Meuser

House Vaks

058 C

6 Aharonovich Street
[A] L. Liebman
1937

This building is comprised of three storeys raised on top of *piloti* on the ground floor. It is located on a corner plot, and its circulation core is accessed via two separate entrances, each facing a different street. In order to soften the sternness of the façade and to fuse the building volume to the urban fabric, the corner pointing toward the crossroad was rounded. Beside strengthening the building's horizontal aspect, the combination of recessed and projected balconies grants the façade an interesting quality and accentuates the play of light and shadow. Between 1938 and 1939, one of the apartments in the building was used as the headquarter for the HaEtzel resistance movement. One day prior to the beginning of the Second World War, the headquarter was raided and the members arrested. During the early 1940s, after a bombardment of Tel Aviv by Italian aeroplanes, shelter walls were built on the ground floor. The added walls decreased the quality of the wide entrance lobby drastically, yet they remind us of the city's history.

Philipp Meuser

Philipp Meuser

House Kit

059 C

4 Aharonovich Street
[A] Dr. Robert Hoff
[R] Eyal Ziv Architects
1939

The free space on the *piloti* level of this building lightens its appearance and creates a naturally ventilated public space for its residents. The irregularly shaped, triangular corner plot on which the building stands produced a jagged façade, which was exploited to generate a clear separation between the individual apartments, thus allowing maximum privacy to the residents. As was costumary to other buildings designed in the late 1930s, the circulation core is located at the centre of the building and does not show on any of its façades. The stairway is accessed via an impressive stone and marble entrance hall that is accessed through the *piloti* level. The building is covered with varying types of plaster. The façades facing the streets are covered with coarse scratch plaster while the back façades feature a smoother plaster and the pillars on the ground floor are covered with stone plaster. In 1940, one year after the building was completed, it was damaged by bombs from Italian aeroplanes. Shortly thereafter, it was renovated and the walls were reinforced. The building was released for renovation under strict preservation regulations and refurbished in 2014. The changes included a new, recessed top floor, which is barely visible from street level. It is recommended to visit the lobby with its subtly designed Terrazzo flooring, including the raised platform at its centre with its rounded door.

Philipp Meuser

Philipp Meuser

Philipp Meuser

Itzhak Kalter

House Gerber, Rubin and Shapir

060 C

42-44 Chovevei Zion Street
[A] Y. Kamenitzky, H. Blumenfeld
1936

Yael Schmidt

A prominent aspect of the International Style in Tel Aviv is the significant expansion of green spaces. Part of each project was to create gardens that serve as a buffer zone between the public and private domains. Built on a joint plot, this U-shaped house features a semi-private garden for its residents, which functions as the heart of the building and includes a fountain in its centre. The fountain is plated in green and turquoise tiles, which ties it to the garden's lush greenery. It is recommended to enter and inspect the garden area. The building features two circulation cores with round windows, and the sides of the small extruded pedestal are also clad with glass tiles. The façade features two different kinds of exposed aggregate plaster with different colouring. In order to emphasise horizontality, each storey is highlighted by a bold, outward projecting band that is covered with a dark coloured plaster.

Philipp Meuser

Philipp Meuser

House Tiroshin-Finkelstein/ House Rivkind

061 C

51/53 Chovevei Zion Street
[A] Shlomo Gepstein, Yaakov Ginzburg
1937/1936

Philipp Meuser

These two adjacent residential buildings share a similar design despite being built separately and designed by two different architects. Each of the buildings is composed of a ground floor with storage areas for its residents and three residential storeys on top. Both buildings share the same shape, apartment orientation, and balconies design. In addition, similar decorative elements can be spotted on their façades, such as the projected concrete frames surrounding the balconies. The main difference between the two buildings is the design of the entrance areas on the ground floor. While House Rivkin features a plain and straight-forward entrance, neighbouring House Tiroshin-Finkelstein includes a recessed entrance which forms a small garden between the *piloti* in a similar fashion to other buildings in the area. The wall at the entrance is clad with greenish tiles, and the front garden includes a stone bench with the same greenish tint. The garden also includes a fountain and flower beds with local sandstone borders. On the other hand, notice the usage of natural colours in the lobby of House Tiroshin-Finkelstein, creating a transition from the interior to the exterior space as is typical for the local modernist buildings.

Yael Schmidt

53 Chovevei Zion Street

Philipp Meuser

53 Chovevei Zion Street

Philipp Meuser

51 Chovevei Zion Street

Philipp Meuser

Philipp Meuser

51 Chovevei Zion Street

Philipp Meuser

House Galili

062 C

63 Chovevei Zion Street
[A] Dr. Robert Hoff, Eng. E. Ginzburg
1936

This relatively standard building features an impressive entry space as befits the time and area in which it was constructed. The building is composed of a ground floor below three residential floors, each comprising three apartments. Originally, the ground floor included a garage that was altered to function as a small store in spite of the fact that the municipality had restricted the operation of commercial functions in small residential streets. As the modification contradicted the municipal guidelines it was restored to its original function later. The building's entrance is raised above street level and is accessed through the garden area. The entry hall features a chequered, black and white patterned Terrazzo flooring and a wide stairway with matching, monochromatic colouring. Built-in garden beds and benches adorn the entrance hall. The elevated platform originally featured a unique ceiling lighting solution that was, however, abandoned later, and a curved wall with glass brick openings.

Philipp Meuser

Philipp Meuser

House Mirenburg

063 C

65 Chovevei Zion Street
[A] Pinchas (Philip) Hütt
1935

This relatively large building is located on a sharp-edged plot which dictates its shape. It is composed as a cluster of three building volumes, which are arranged such that they form a U-shaped building with a gradually fragmented façade. The composition of the fragmented volumes generates a small front garden for the residents. A semi-cylindrical building volume projects from the central volume, which ties the façade to the urban setting that surrounds it. The curved volume features balconies and concrete aprons that stretch across its entire length and accentuate the building's horizontal orientation. The fragmentation of the building volume allows each apartment to be exposed to three cardinal directions, thus allowing the flow of natural ventilation. The front façade is covered with exposed aggregate plaster mixed with small basalt chips. Most of the building is composed of simple forms, although when looking closely you can spot one ornament: the balcony drainage pipes on the second floor are eagle-shaped.

Denis Esakov

Itzhak Kalter

House Tovim

064 C

2 Dov Hoz Street
[A] Nachum Zelkind
[R] Arcod Architects
1934

This building is located on a corner plot overlooking the intersection of three residential streets which generates numerous perspectives. The design takes this parameter into consideration, resulting in a three-dimensional façade which incorporates recessed and projecting balconies, concrete shading canopies and irregularities of the façade in general, all measures to create a lush play of light and shadow. The building was renovated in 1995. An elevator shaft was added in the backyard, and a recessed storey with two additional apartments was added on the roof. The top floor was designed with a curved corrugated roof which extends across the entire length of the building. The new element was intentionally designed to contrast the modernistic straight lines, originating from the belief that the contrast would serve to honour the past and simultaneously acknowledging the future, making the building modern and post-modern at the same time.

Philipp Meuser

Doron Pinchas

Philipp Meuser

House Tzimbel

065 C

8 Dov Hoz Street
[A] Ben-Ami Shulman
1935

Itzhak Kalter

House Tzimbel is a three-storey residential building with two apartments on each of its floors, and a basement floor which includes storage space and a residential unit. Its plot's dimensions and orientation towards the west present an optimal apartment layout in relation to the western sea breeze which allows sufficient natural ventilation. Since it was built relatively early and unlike most of the buildings in the area, this house does not include an entrance lobby. Its horizontal emphasis is articulated by elongated balconies with unique metal railings. The horizontality is interrupted by the vertical thermometer window. This building went through many informal additions and alterations, and, today, is in a derelict state that renders the original building's appearance almost invisible.

Philipp Meuser

Philipp Meuser

Itzhak Kalter

Cooperative Housing Estates D, E, F (Me'onot Hod)

066 C

Frug 11-15, Freshman 33-35, Dov Hoz 10-14
[A] Arieh Sharon
1934

These cooperative housing estates were the second to be realised in Tel Aviv. Architect Arieh Sharon started his career planning buildings for Kibbutz Gan-Shmuel, of which he was also one of the founders. He then studied at the Bauhaus school in Dessau under second principal Hannes Meyer, who held strong socialist beliefs. Cooperative conviction and the aesthetic language of the modernist Avantgarde converged in Sharon's work. As such, Sharon was the ideal planner for cooperative dwellings like this one. It is possible that the estate design was influenced by the *Zeilenblock* building designed by Mies van der Rohe for the Weissenhof Estate in 1927, that Sharon visited as part of his studies. Unlike its predecessors, this housing estate was designed as a block building with a fragmented façade that follows the articulation of the streets on which they stand. Sharon fought the municipal bureaucracy for permission to change the parcellation layout of the original plot design in order to realise the building block he envisioned. Each of the circulation cores serves six apartments and features a street and a courtyard entrance. The central building (estate E) is shaped like a large U, which engulfs a large, communal courtyard. The courtyard entrance faces Frishman Street and is accessed through a piloti level leading to a stairway which mediates the topographic difference between the courtyard and the street. The buildings with the relatively small apartments were to provide communal solutions for the everyday needs of its dwellers. Thus, the ground floor comprised a kindergarten, sanitary facilities, and commercial spaces. Nowadays, the building's appearance has changed slightly. Some of the small balconies which follow the width of the openings were demolished to be replaced by longer ones, while some were closed in order to enlarge the apartments' footprint. The large stairway windows, which allowed for natural ventilation, were replaced by smaller ones.

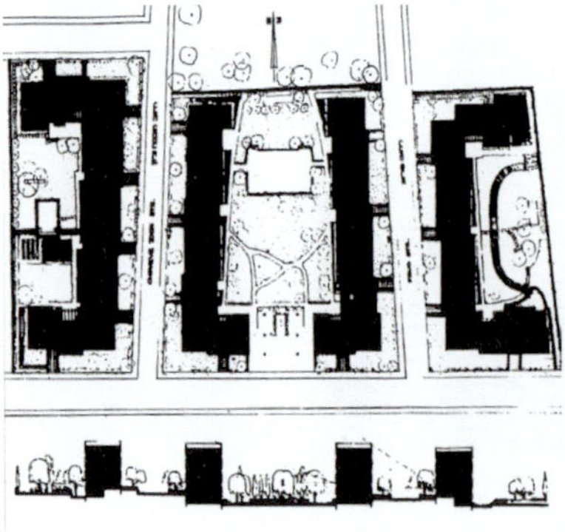

Municipal Archive

Itzhak Kalter

Philipp Meuser

Philipp Meuser

House Zeiroth Mizrachi

067 C

16-18 Dov Hoz Street
[A] Yitzchak Reich, Yaakov Ben-Sira (Shiffman)
[R] Tsionov-Vitkon Architects
1938

This building was designed to serve as a boarding school and educational institution for religious girls. It was established by the Mizrachi Women's Organisation, which was a branch of HaMizrachi, the Religious Zionist of America organisation, who supported the Zionist enterprise in Mandatory Palestine. The plot was donated, and the building was funded by Yaakov Gesundheit, a Zionist philanthropist who was a member of HaMizrachi. Like many other public buildings of that time, the planning was done by Yaakov Shifman who was the city architect and responsible for the regulations permitting only buildings of the International Style, in collaboration with his deputy Yitzhak Reich. This L-shaped building was built on joined plots that were leveled below the street height. It was originally composed of a ground floor and two upper storeys, but a few years after its construction a third floor was added. The inner façade facing the courtyard is characterized by its continuous balustrades which stretches across its entire length.

The original function of the building was abandoned in the 1970s, and the building served varying educational functions until 1999, from which time onward is stood vacant. At the time of the social protests of 2011, after many years of neglect, it housed various illegal residents and informal activities. The building was occupied by protesters who demanded it to be renovated and assigned a public program. The City of Tel Aviv, who owns the building, has conceded to this grass-roots protest and changed the function into a community centre, designed in collaboration with the public. In 2015, despite not being listed for preservation like many other public International Style buildings, Zeiroth Mizrachi was renovated to reinstate its original appearance. The building now hosts a kindergarten, a café, community workspaces and more.

Dror Einav

Philipp Meuser

C

Philipp Meuser

House Rabinovich
41 Frishman Street
[A] Ben-Ami Shulman
1935

068 C

House Rabinovich was designed for a mixed residential-commercial functionality on the side facing Dizengoff Street, and a contrasting residential area facing Frishman Street. The architect put great emphasis on this separation, granting each façade a unique appeal. The façade facing Dizengoff Street is emphasised by two pro-jecting cylindrical volumes, while the façade facing Frishman Street expresses a dynamic flow towards the east. Many alterations of the building have resulted in less of a differentiation between the two façades; commercial spaces were installed on the ground floor of the south façade, and a third storey was added. Despite the damaging interventions to the building, the architect's playful approach to the possibilities of building with reinforced concrete can still be seen when looking at the corners of the façades on Dizengoff Street.

Zolatan Kluger

Itzhak Kalter

Philipp Meuser

Itzhak Kalter

House Haller

069 C

49 Frishman Street

[A] Benjamin Anekstein

1936

Unlike other buildings in the area, House Haller does not present an impressive lobby or a courtyard to serve as a buffer between the urban landscape and the estate itself, and its entrance is marked only by two round pillars. It demonstrates the plasticity of pure volumes as befits the International Style. The building volume that houses the residential units is slightly projected outwards from the façade, which bears a clear horizontal emphasis. Despite the fact that the façade does have some load-bearing function, the architect integrated ribbon-like windows which are recessed in relation to the projected area, creating the impression of continuity along the openings. The narrow façade facing Reines Street features recessed balconies which cast shadows onto the building itself. The roof was designed with a concrete pergola which is noticeable along its façades and further accentuate sits horizontal articulation as well as shading the communal roof.

Philipp Meuser

Philipp Meuser

Philipp Meuser

House Pechthold

070 C

13-15 Ester Hamalka Street
[A] Eng. Tzvi Pechthold
[R] Alon Ben Nun Architects
1936

This relatively large residential building was built on two combined parcels. It was split into three different sections, each of which with its own entrance. The building used to comprise a communal courtyard, articulated by the building's U-shape. As common to buildings of the same style, the floor plan envisioned a functional division of the apartments with living rooms facing the front façades, and sanitary and service areas facing the inner courtyard. In 2017, the building was renovated, adding 1000 square metres to the existing space. One added storey is finished similarly to the original building with only small details disenchanting the new storey from the original ones. Another storey on top is recessed from the main façade and features entirely different materiality to preserve the proportions of the original design. The courtyard now serves a different function; a patio with a new elevator functions as the lobby area and main circulation core.

Philipp Meuser

Philipp Meuser

Ruth Garden

071 C

Ruth, Shulamit, Yael,
Esther HaMalka Streets
[A] Sir Patrick Geddes
1927-1929

This garden is an example of the typical pocket garden that was part of Sir Patrick Geddes' city plan that he developed for Tel Aviv in 1925. This visionary plan designed by the Scottish garden planner defines the basic structure of the city by determining the relationship between the built structures and their surrounding landscape, and thus between the city's denizens and their environment. The fusion of the built urban fabric with green public spaces took into consideration the physical, economic, social and human needs of society, all based on an environmental approach. Geddes' most important achievement was the invention of the "superblock", created to serve the civic education of the new society. This education was supposed to form certain desirable behavioural patterns in the residential block. From a mere planning perspective, the block structure allowed for zoning of the city's orthogonal grid in a hierarchical structure. Outside these "home blocks", large "main ways" served public transportation and commerce, while narrower "home ways" (quiet side streets) created intimacy and tranquility. The centre of the home blocks typically featured either a garden or a public institution. By creating such patterns of nesting cells, Geddes defined the relationship between humans and nature, between society and culture, as a precondition to convert his ideas into social processes. Ruth Garden was one of the first gardens to be designed between a cluster of residential streets. It is a good example of the urban design approach for the city of the time, namely, to establish main streets which split off into quieter secondary streets. The streets surrounding the garden are all one-way streets that do not invite traffic to pass through them and that are therefore very quiet. The garden at the center of their intersection creates an island of tranquillity right in the heart of the declared UNESCO World Heritage site, parallel to Dizengoff Square, one of Tel Aviv's busiest places. Just as Sir Patrick Geddes originally intended, the green space still provides a quiet retreat from the hectic urban lifestyle today.

Philipp Meuser

Philipp Meuser

C

Yael Schmidt

House Pashkovski

072 C

4 Ruth Street
[A] Dr. Robert Hoff
1939

This building is a good example of International Style residential building typology that evolved in the latter part of the 1930s. It is composed of a simple rectangular building volume with a circulation core located in the centre of the mass, and not at the façade as was common in comparable, earlier buildings. The ceilings on the building's rear side are raised by half a storey over the ones in the front. The ground floor is recessed to make space for an open space supported by *piloti*, showing the influence of Le Corbusier. The thus created front garden grants access to the staircase. The garden features a small pond and sitting area and leads to an impressive entrance hall adorned with stone tiling and Art Deco influenced, decorative elements. The space still features some of the original details from the 1930s, and the luxurious entrance area reflects the affluent status of its residents.

Yael Schmidt

Philipp Meuser

House Dunklblum

073 C

3 Yael Street
[A] Oskar Kaufmann
1935

Oskar Kaufmann was Germany's leading theatre architect of the 1920s. Among his works are the Volksbühne in Berlin and many others. Kaufmann originally emigrated to Palestine in order to build the National Habima Theatre. House Dunkelblum is the only residential building designed by Kaufmann in Tel Aviv. Due to the local restrictions to build only in the International Style, Kaufmann shifted from Expressionism to Modernism, resulting in a unique architectural language combining the two styles. The building stands on a podium-like platform overlooking the nearby Shulamit Garden. Its theatre-like entrance is composed of two mirroring sets of stairs that lead to the elevated podium and a door that grants access to the building's lobby and main circulation core. The entrance is set back from the building line and forms a convex protrusion with a subtracted concave in its lower part, which makes for a dramatic entrance. The building volume is composed of a rectangular mass with rounded edges. The façade is only interrupted by convexly curved windows and protruding balconies, some of which were closed over the years. The façades facing the street feature a decorative flowery plaster, an extraordinary feature on this building. The projecting balconies are distinguished from the main building volume by their contrasting smooth, white coating. The architect has designed every detail of the building, from the railings to the lamps, in a way that it results in a true total work of art.

Courtesy of the Gorne

Philipp Meuser

Philipp Meuser

Philipp Meuser

House Rosenwasser

074 C

5 Yael Street
[A] Yehuda Fogel, Shlomo Mekori
1936

House Rosenwasser's maritime motifs such as the round windows and ships-deck-like balconies were common elements in the design of the International Style. The goal was to symbolize a global attitude unrestrained by any one culture. The façade features two separate entrances leading the building's circulation cores. Each entrance is clad with square brown tiles that were probably imported from Germany at the time of the transfer agreement (see Introduction). The protruding balconies located on either side of the main staircases have a semicircular shape with decoratively ornamented railings, which grants the building its streamlined appearance. In contrast to the expressive balconies on the front façade, the building's sides feature balconies designed with a more cubistic approach. Their railings protrude from the building volume and they incorporate sun protection. Over the years, some of the balconies were closed off in order to expand the footprint of individual apartments. It is recommended to go inside the building to see unique handrails in the staircase.

C

Philipp Meuser

House Pashitski

075 C

12 Shlomo Hamelech Street
[A] Y . Klugman in collaboration with Pinchas (Philip) Hütt
1935

In order to soften the appearance of the sharp angles of the plot, the architects rounded the corners of House Pashitski, granting it a streamlined appeal as was common to Erich Mendelsohn's International Style buildings. The rounded corner creates a flowing continuity between the two intersecting streets on which it stands. The building exhibits accentuated horizontality derived from a composition combining protruding and recessed balconies, concrete shading cornices, and slightly recessed, horizontal stripes marking the vertical boundaries of the windows. The top of the building was characterised by an exaggerated, cantilevered cornice that was, however, later removed. Common to the International Style, the building features a unique thermometer window. Although House Pashitski was originally built for residential purposes only, it now hosts a café, an ideal place to take a break since the coffee there tastes exceptionally good.

Philipp Meuser

Philipp Meuser

Philipp Meuser

The Urban Fringe

Philipp Meuser

Yael Schmidt

Beyond the World Cultural Heritage

This tour will take you east, then south of Tel Aviv's main artery, exploring the outer edges of the declared UNESCO heritage zone. Although some of the sites on the tour are not masterpieces of modernistic architecture, they convey the spirit of the urban landscape and show the entire mix of architectural typologies that characterise Tel Aviv. The second part of the tour leads through the up-and-coming Florentin neighbourhood, which is situated in the south of Tel Aviv. It was established in 1927 south of the Jaffa-Jerusalem railway line on the site of a former, extensive orchard. The quarter was founded by immigrants from Thessaloniki, Greece, who designed it as a bourgeois neighbourhood that combines craft, small industry, and commerce. The cityscape is characterised by three to four storey-high buildings along narrow streets, resulting in a relatively high-density neighbourhood. In the wake of the economic crisis during the Second World War and with the development of the Geddes plan towards the north of the city, the Florentin neighbourhood became home to migrants from Poland, Turkey, Yemen, Iraq, and Egypt, who lived there in poor conditions which inevitably led to suffering from social and hygienic problems. Until some time ago, the only reason to visit the neighbourhood was perhaps to get the upholstery on one's living room sofa renewed. But in 1991 a transition occurred; the municipality formulated a plan for renewal that attracted young people to move to the neighbourhood. Significantly lower prices than those in the city centre gave the area a distinctly different character. The combination of workshops and residential housing attracted graffiti artists who used the walls of the neighbourhood as a platform for large works of art. In this neighbourhood, the building style has developed its own architecture language; the "Florentin Style". Unlike in the centre of Tel Aviv, here, the buildings are attached to each other as opposed to free-standing. Their front façades are in-line with the sidewalk without leaving space for a front garden area, creating a block-like appearance. The UNESCO World Cultural Heritage zone does not include this area, which is why different preservation laws apply that mainly refer to the façades and the preservation of the local urban fabric. The basic building typology consists of a relatively high commercial floor, a homogeneous façade with protruding balconies, oriels, and rounded balconies in the street corners, minor decorations like cornices, steel balustrades and thermometer windows. The building styles vary from Eclectic to Art Deco to International Style, whereas a great number of new constructions feature curtain wall façades. The DNA of the neighbourhood and its genius loci still reflect the original division of the streets according to the type of commerce and products that they accommodated. There is a spice street, a toy street, streets for garments. All of which are still intertwined with the everyday life of the neighbourhood. Today, Florentin offers some of the city's most prominent attractions – (vegan) food, nightlife, and a humble art scene. Therefore, this tour not only introduces you to the local architecture but also presents a neighbourhood that has reinvented itself into an interesting and attractive place to explore.

Six-floor residential building on 73 Shalma Street

Irmel Kamp-Bandau

House Delfiner - Picker

076 D

51 Mazeh Street
[A] Zeev (Wilhelm) Heller
[R] Tal Eyal Architects
1933

This impressive U-shaped corner building ensemble sits on two adjacent plots and comprises of two connected buildings. Each of the buildings' three floors contain five apartements of varying size. The building's front façade is rounded at the corner, thus creating a dynamic feel which weaves the two street fronts together. To further emphasise the building ensemble's corner location, two Mexican Washingtonia palm trees were planted in front of the corner curve of the façade. The front façade's appearance is characterised by restrained three-dimensionality, achieved with long, ribbon-like, recessed balconies, the "free corner", and the symmetrical, semi-circle protrusions. The building's horizontality is emphasised by ribbons of apertures, sunken balconies, and the use of differently coloured exposed aggregate plaster. Each ribbon balcony is shared by two apartments, a common design feature of a time that promoted communal values. However, archival photos show that separations were installed a short time after the building was complete. The building's front façade is built close to the plot's boundaries in order to create a monumental appearance, but, more importantly, to allow for a large garden on the rear side. The building was renovated in 2014, and its backyard was converted to serve as a parking lot.

Philipp Meuser

Itzhak Kalter

House Ha'aretz

077 D

56 Mazeh Street
[A] Joseph and Zeev Berlin
[R] Akiva Lomnitz
1933, 1996

This building used to house the headquarters and print facilities of the Haaretz Newspaper, one of the first Jewish newspapers at the time of the British mandate, still published today. The building was designed in the simplistic and functional fashion that was common to International Style industrial buildings; even though a rather rare typology in Tel Aviv at that time. Since the north facing façade was not exposed to direct sunlight, the architects were less restrained in terms of the size of the window openings and designed them following the typical European style. The asymmetrical façade was composed of wide window openings, an entrance at the western part of the building, and a staircase window resembling that of Walter Gropius' famous Fagus Factory. Three years after the building was completed, a long balcony and a cornice were added to soften the harsh appearance of the façade.

The entrance features a curved wall that accentuates the stairway's window and its independence from the building's construction. The original building included two storeys, the ground floor housed storage and printing facilities, and the upper floor the editorial board. As the years passed, a basement was added to provide storage underneath the building. In 1990, many years after the newspaper's headquarters had moved to a bigger building in the city's southern part, the building was demolished. Later, the front part was reconstructed, and a hotel was built in the rear part as well as the adjoining plot to the west. Today, the building houses a boutique hotel.

Philipp Meuser

Philipp Meuser

Philipp Meuser

Philipp Meuser

Itzhak Kalter

D

Cooperative Housing Estates A, B, C

078 D

63-65, 62, 64 -67 Maze Street
[A] Dov Kochinski,
[R] Yonatan Schlein, Arieh Sharon
1931-1933

These cooperative housing estates are the first example of urban cooperative housing in Mandatory Palestine, which evolved to be one of the most common typologies of the Zionist project before the foundation of the State of Israel. This complex was built in three stages, while each stage included the construction of two buildings. The three projects were built following a comb-shaped design, in which the buildings stand perpendicularly to the street so that their main façades face a communal inner garden that is intended for the residents' use, while its secondary façades the street. The broad façades are oriented on a west-east axis, allowing maximum exposure of the apartments to natural ventilation flowing from the west. Initially, there were struggles to find occupants for this complex. The urban workers who believed in the Zionist ideas of working the land dreamed of an agrarian lifestyle were not inclined to settle in the city centre. The centre for cooperative housing had to send representatives to factories in order to convince workers to purchase an apartment in the complex. After the success of the pilot, many workers saw it fit and demanded the construction of additional cooperative housing in Tel Aviv, Jerusalem, and Haifa. An additional floor was added to two of the buildings (65-67 Maze street), resulting in significant harm to the overall proportions of the building. The new buildings' height undermined the relationship between the width of the inner gardens and the building volumes. The area in which the complex stands used to be a part of an old Templer farm. The walls surrounding the farm were made of local limestone and are still visible today.

Philipp Meuser

Philipp Meuser

House Leon Recanati

079 D

79 Mazeh Street
[A] Yaakov Orenstein, Shlomo Liakovski
[R] Bar-Orian Architects
1935

This U-shaped residential building houses commercial functions on the front side and mixed use in the remainder of the ground floor. The upper storeys are designed for residential use, an overall composition that was atypical for the period of the 1930. The U-shape of the building offers good ventilation and opening areas for the apartments, and also a small garden for the residents' use. Its peculiar form originates from the right-angled, trapezoid shaped plot, which is dictated by Menachem Begin Road. The street was constructed in the 19th century, connecting Jaffa and Petach Tikva at the outskirts of the city. The areas to the southeast were specified to function as commercial and industrial zones, hence the building's south-east facing, commercial façade. The separation of residential and commercial functions is very coherent, as the entrances to the residential part of the building are located on its northern façade, facing Maze Street. The building's commercial front can only be accessed via Menachem Begin Road, the building's morphology further accentuates this separation. The ground floor portion of the façade features a diagonal glass and concrete wall. On the first floor, the façade protrudes to function as parapets for the balconies. The residential area facing Menachem Begin Road is characterised by an orthogonal, stepped, jagged façade with a 4.5-metre-long repetitive pattern. To soften its jaggedness, round balconies and shading elements were incorporated on the second floor. The added balconies create fluidity along the sternly fragmented façade and further differentiate its morphological properties, thus creating an interesting play of light and shadow. This building demonstrates how two very different constructive programs can be woven together to form one complex and advanced unit. In 2000, the building was renovated to follow the original design.

Philipp Meuser

Irmel Kamp-Bandau

Irmel Kamp-Bandau

House Gavrilovich

080 D

64 Nachmani Street

[A] Joseph Kashdan

1936

The shape of this building is derived from the sharp angle created by the intersection of Nachmani Street and Menachem Begin Road, designed with an ideal length for a row of commercial spaces. The building is composed of two building volumes, one of which is long and rectangular and the other cubic. The rounded edge located at the plot's edge connects the two volumes and softens the harshness of the sharp-angled plot. The south-eastern façade faces Menachem Begin Road. It features a commercial zone on the ground floor and a residential zone on the upper floors. The façade's horizontal aspect is accentuated by wide apertures, long shading cornices, and protruding, round balconies. Each of the streets adjacent to the building features an entrance to the residential areas. The south-eastern entrance is composed of a plain door that is embedded between two storefronts, while the northern entrance facing Nachmani Street is characterised by complex three-dimensionality with a convex void visually set apart from the cubic volume. The commercial space is separated from the rest of the building by a wide cornice that expands from the southern part of the façade to the building's northern entrance. The spaces designated for commercial use feature heightened ceilings, creating a height difference between residential spaces in the building's northern part. It is recommended to examine the building's entrance facing Nachmani Street.

Philipp Meuser

Zoltan Kluger

Max Fein Technical School

081 D

15 David Khakhami Street
[A] Erich Mendelsohn, Eng. Erich Kampinski
1935

Max Fein Technical School was designed by architect Erich Mendelsohn, the developer of the dynamic functionalism of Modernism. He was one of the most influential architects of the International Style in the world and, specifically, in Israel. Although Mendelsohn never personally signed the official submission for the permit at the municipality, it is assumed that he was responsible for the primary design. The building is a former training school for technical professions, located on the eastern outskirts of the city. The school building is composed of a simple rectangular building volume that is penetrated by rows of relatively small windows. Even though the apertures are oriented vertically, the short distance from one window to the next in addition to their repetitiveness creates a ribbon with a clear horizontal emphasis. The first two floors served as workshops, while the top floor housed classrooms. All rooms were grouped around the inner core, which functioned as a courtyard and allowed for short distances between the individual locations. Originally, the building featured a rounded balcony on the second-floor level of the front façades, which is a signature item that reappears in other designs created by Mendelsohn. Max Fein Technical School was hit during an Egyptian airstrike in 1948 and underwent fundamental changes over the years.

Philipp Meuser

Philipp Meuser

Itzhak Kalter

House Hadar - Citrus House 082 D

22 HaRakevet Street

[A] Carl Rubin

1935

This office building's design was the winning entry of a competition that was commissioned by the Hadar Company for their headquarters (Hadar: Hebrew for citrus). It was the first building in the city to be built with a steel-frame structure in that period. Due to its central location in proximity to the old train station, the building was mostly at full office occupancy along the years. The U-shaped building is composed of a cluster of volumes of which the main volume protrudes towards the intersection on which it stands. The building's horizontal aspect is primarily due to ribbon windows. The curved façade is strongly influenced by architect Erich Mendelsohn in whose office Carl Rubin had worked in Germany. Although the facade isn't free of constructive value, the columns, which are located along the windows, are recessed from the remainder of the façade and not coated with exposed aggregate plaster, creating an interpretation of the ribbon window concept. Originally, the building was three to four storeys high, but in the 1950s an additional floor was added to each of its wings, destructing the original proportions. Additionally, many of the original window frames were replaced over the years, which an even greater loss of the original appearance. During the peak of World War II, in 1941, the building was confiscated by the British Mandate Rule to function as a part of a military base. The British established a judiciary facility in the building, accommodating a court of law and intelligence services, resulting in hostility from the Yeshuv (a nickname for the Hebrew Jewish community in Mandatory Palestine). The building was repeatedly attacked by Zionist paramilitary resistance groups. The most serious attack on the building was conducted by the underground organisation Etzel; bombardment inside the building lasted for days. In order to carry out the operation, a tunnel was dug from an adjacent building, for the target building was surrounded by barbed wire and therefore inaccessible. It is assumed that members of the resistance organisation Haganah detected the tunnel and wanted to disclose the fact. Members of Etzel, enemies to Haganah, thereupon closed the tunnel in order to destroy it, an action which resulted in the death of one Haganah member. This incident shook the Jewish community. After the end of the British Mandate, the building was returned to its original function.

Itzhak Kalter

Philipp Meuser

Philipp Meuser

Irmel Kamp-Bandau

House Vilozni

083 D

23 Mikve Israel Street
[A] Mordechai Rosengarten
[R] Yaniv Pardo Architects
1936-1938

House Vilozni is a corner building that combines commercial functions on the ground floor and residential functions on the two upper levels. Its relatively large size highlights the fact that the neighbourhood underwent changes as a result of the city's expansion towards the east. The building is a combination of a U and an L-shape. The main, rectangular building volume sits in the middle of the parcel, recessed from the street, while the shape of the side façade creates a small plaza in the front. There is a small garden in the rear of the parcel. The building's most prominent feature are its elongated balconies which follow a strictly horizontal line. The balustrade stretches across the main façade and protrudes beyond both sides, creating continuity a dynamic feel. In order to further accentuate horizontality, the banisters were designed with fragmented, horizontal lines that create a play of light and shadow. Today, the building is subject to strict preservation regulations, which only allow the addition of a recessed roof apartment.

Yaniv Pardo Architects

House Jacobson

084 D

28 Levontin Street
[A] Emanuel Halbrecht
[R] Nitza Metzger Szmuk
1937

Originally, this residential-commercial building was built to accommodate commercial trade on the ground floor and office spaces on the upper floors. However, shortly after its construction, some of the offices were turned into apartments. The ensemble comprises three main building volumes, arranged in a U-shape that enclose a courtyard facing east. Every intersection between the building volumes marks the location of a circulation core. The main entrance is distinguished by its corner location and the unique staircase windows. The generously wide staircase features green Terrazzo stairs and walls clad with yellow tiles. Sufficient natural light enters this space through south and north oriented windows. As common to buildings built in the second part of the 1930s, this house features many meticulously crafted decorative elements, representing the wealth of its owners. The ground floor is surfaced with light-coloured, local stone, the entrances are framed with red stone, and the handrails, lattices, and gates demonstrate impressive metalwork. In 2012, the building was renovated by architect Nitza Metzger Szmuk under strict preservation regulations.

Philipp Meuser

Itzhak Kalter

Irmel Kamp-Bandau

House Levy

085 D

11 Levontin Street
[A] E. Ginzburg, Dr. Robert Hoff
1937

House Levy houses commercial spaces on the ground floor and three apartments on each of the upper floors. The floor-plans of the apartments go conform with the common formula of the International Style, where the main living rooms face the street and functional rooms and sanitary facilities are oriented towards the building's backyard. The main façade, which is also the building's longest plane, overlooks HaSharon Garden. The horizontal emphasis is achieved by recessed balconies and apertures. The upper part of the balustrade is cantilevered over the façade and generates a horizontal shadow line. As common to other buildings of that time, the building's only vertical element is the thermometer window in the staircase, which, however, creates a subtle fusion between the horizontal and vertical geometries. Despite its clear vertical orientation, the window's metal frames create horizontal modules, that only by being stacked on top of each other form the vertical window.

Philipp Meuser

D

Philipp Meuser

House Furdhaus

086 D

4 HaChashmal Street
[A] Eng. Moshe Karasik (2nd Phase)
[R] Meira Mor Architects
Early 1920s/1934

This building was originally built as a one-storey residential building in the Eclectic Style and was one of the first houses to be erected in the Ramat HaSharon neighbourhood. It was renovated in 1934, with two additional storeys, the ground floor was converted to serve commercial functions, and its style was changed to match the International Style. The shift marks the changes the neighbourhood went through since its inception. As was common to the International Style, the building's façade is asymmetrical and shows how horizontal and vertical elements were integrated at a precise ratio. The building's most prominent element is a unique corner window in the staircase, designed in Art Deco, which starts above the ground floor and at the upper end merges into a roof pergola. The separation between commercial and residential functions is emphasised by an L-shaped concrete cornice that starts above the ground floor and connects to the first floor's balcony. The building was renovated again in 2017 and returned to its original form.

Irmel Kamp-Bandau

Philipp Meuser

G. Eric and Edith Matson Photograph Collection, Library of Congress

House Moyal 087 D

138-140 Allenby Street
[A] Eng. D. Tuvia, Hillel Shlush
[R] Arcod Architects
1931, 1935

House Moyal is located in the vicinity of Kikar HaMoshavot (Hebrew for Square of the Settlements), one of Tel Aviv's most important squares, where several urban axes meet that connect Jaffa and Tel Aviv to the Jewish settlements of the northern Sharon plain. This building was constructed as a one-storey, commercial building including retail and storage space. Its original Art Deco façade was composed of glass and wood cladding. After Tel Aviv's business centre had been established, the owners decided to expand it by two additional office storeys. The expansion resulted in a stylistic shift and its original ground floor façade was stripped of ornamentation. The floor plans of the added floors originated from the layout of the original building and were designed with clean geometry including ribbon openings and elongated balconies with no decorative value. One of the building's corners is accentuated by a concrete frame and white-coloured plaster, contrasting with the grey pigment of the rest of the façade. In 1963, the building underwent renovation another time in order to expand the office space and introduce an elevator system. A third office floor was added with an additional external circulation core at the rear side of the plot.

Arcod Architects

Shay Epstein

Shay Epstein

Shay Epstein

House Carasso
34 Jaffa Street
[A] Arieh Cohen
1939

088 D

This mixed-use building's ground floor accommodates 19 commercial spaces with storage areas. Each of its two upper storeys includes 33 office units. The building is U-shaped and surrounds an inner courtyard. It is bordered by three streets and marks the end of the block in which it is located. Accordingly, it has rounded corners to convey dynamism and to reflect the shape the urban land-scape. The south sides of both façades facing HaMashbir Street and Herzl Street conclude in a slightly projected volume. Each of these sections of the building includes a stairway which stretches all the way to the roof in addition to the main stairway, which is accessed through the façade facing Jaffa Road. The building has a distinct horizontal articulation as a result of its elongated ribbon window openings, its gallery windows, and a cornice which separates the commercial functions from its office functions. In their original form, the ribbon windows were designed in a fashion that was very common to Tel Aviv's International Style: as an open, continuous balcony with a concrete apron above it providing shade. However, over the years the openings were closed and the building lost its coherent appearance. Take a look at the building's generous stairway that can be accessed via HaMashbir Street.

Sharon Golan Yaron

Irmel Kamp-Bandau

Sharon Golan Yaron

Rudi Weissenstein

House Romano

089 D

7-9 Jaffa Road
[A] Meir Hormann, Binyamin Anekstein
1947

This building was built as Tel Aviv's first shopping mall. Most of the ground floor was taken up by retail clothing stores, while the upper floors originally served office functions. The rectangular building is composed around an impressive courtyard and can be accessed through three different entrances. The first two storeys facing the courtyard feature an arcade of columns, granting entrance to the shops and allowing various relationships between the broad courtyard and the building. When inspecting the façade, its repetition of window openings and the abstraction of details, one can notice that the building was designed during the latter part of Modernism. For the past five years, the house has accommodated mixed functions and also serves as a local cultural centre. During daytime, it is mainly used a wholesale shopping mall, mostly for clothing retailers, while during the night, the young and hip Tel Aviv society frequents the bar, a restaurant, a pizzeria, a record shop, galleries and more.

Philipp Meuser

Philipp Meuser

Ahronskind House

090 D

25 Hakison Street

[A] S. Sorpin, M.Ben Shaul

1933

Typical for the neighbourhood, this residential-commercial building combines the New Objectivity of the International Style with decorative Art Deco elements in the staircase and cornice. The L-shaped floorplan places all the living areas along the façade facing the street and all the functional spaces such as bathrooms and kitchens toward the rear façade facing the backyard. Although the building is a listed monument, there is little appreciation by the owners. The last documentation of this building in the records of the municipal archive from 2013 states that the building poses a public risk, calling for immediate maintenance of the balconies and the upper cornice. A sad example of neglect.

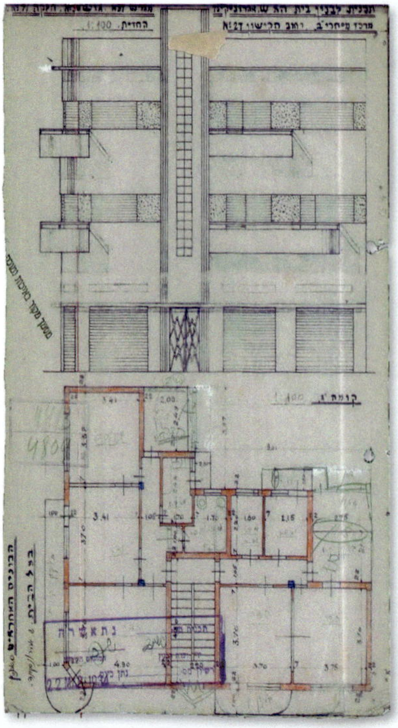

Municipal Archive

Philipp Meuser

Philipp Meuser

House Meshulam
Avadia Carasso

091 D

7 Wolfshon Street
[A] Haim Meshulam
1936

House Meshulam is a residential building that comprises a commercial ground floor and two upper residential storeys. Differently from other International Style buildings in the area, which demonstrate a straight-forward design approach stripped of any unique detailing, this building's façade was meticulously designed and features a design language more similar to buildings constructed in the northern part of the city despite its block building layout. The building's façade has a horizontal accentuation and rounded corners. Circular windows emphasise the style's streamliner motif. Each residential floor contains two apartments of which the eastern units' area is slightly larger and feature an additional room. Initially, the roof served as a communal space for the residents until being closed and altered to function as an additional apartment.

Philipp Meuser

Philipp Meuser

Shalem House
8 Wolfson Street
[A] Yaakov Shiffman
1936

092 D

The curved façade of House Shalem accentuates the corner plot that it sits on. Filigree executed scratch plaster connects the ribbon-like windows, and the horizontal body is broken up by the vertical element of the stairway window. The ground floors are reserved for commercial functions as is typical for this neighbourhood. They feature extremely high ceilings and let natural light penetrate through long ribbon windows in the upper wall areas. The balconies on the first and the upper storey were closed over the years, as were the horizontal ventilation slots in the balustrades. In his capacity as city architect, Yaakov Shiffman, architect of the original building, was responsible for the implementation of the Internation Style in Tel Aviv.

Philipp Meuser

Philipp Meuser

Philipp Meuser

House Morduch

093 D

32 Yedidya Frenkel Street
[A] Dr. Robert Hoff (assumed)
[R] Mester-Gal Architects
1938

This building was originally composed of a commerical ground floor and two upper residential floors. It features a horizontal articulation given by the canopy above the ground floor and the residential units' balconies. These balconies extend around the rounded corner of the building, which creates a dynamic effect. In 2017, the building was renovated, and its height was raised to comprise a total of seven storeys. The new storeys vary from each other in order to create a clear hierarchy. The first additional storey follows the exact outline, design, and materiality of the original floors. The other two additional storeys follow the outline as well but differ in materiality and design. The uppermost added storey is recessed and has a smaller foot, rendering it practically invisible from street level.

Nir Ovadia

Nir Ovadia

Nir Ovadia

Philipp Meuser

Residential Building

094 D

14 Washington Boulevard
[A] Unknown
[R] Amnon Bar Or - Tal Gazit Architects
1936

Amnon Bar Or – Tal Gazit Architects

This building was part of the last block to be built in the Florentin neighbourhood in the 1930s. Its completion marked the end of the primary real estate development in the neighbourhood. It is located on the intersection of Florentin Street and Washington Boulevard, which fills an important urban function as the only green artery in the neighbourhood. The building follows the standard layout of the Florentin building typology, featuring a commercial ground floor with heightened ceilings below a three-storey residential area that is signified by bay windows and balconies, besides sharing a party wall with adjacent building. In order to emphasise its corner location, the architect chose to extend the balconies around the building's rounded corner. The building has been renovated; its original size was altered drastically following the municipality's plan to densify the neighbourhood's built fabric. The new additions can be easily spotted as they are marked by cornices. The vertical expansion of the building meant six additional storeys, four of which follow the outline of the original building and two featuring a smaller, recessed footprint.

Eastward view from the ninth floor

Amnon Bar Or – Tal Gazit Architects

House Leon Nachman 095 D

77 Shalma Road

[A] Unknown

[R] Nitza Metzger Scmuk

1938

The northern side of Shalma Road, where this building stands, marks the southern border of the Florentin neighbourhood. The road is of high urban importance and appears on early maps dating as far back as 1878. Originally, the road was paved in order to connect Jaffa to the then neighbouring village Salama (the road's original name) that was located to the east. Since its inception, commercial and industry buildings have established themselves along the road over the years. This building's most dominant characteristic is its Art Deco influenced façade. Differently from the majority of buildings in the neighbourhood, which display simple and function-oriented designs, the façade of House Nachman features carefully designed details. The symmetrical façade is visually split by vertical ribbons located in the centre, a distinct Art Deco detail. The ribbons turn to be articulated horizontally in order to mark the building's end. The building comprises three residential storeys on top of a commercially used ground floor. The entrance was originally clad with black ceramic tiles, which were, however, for the most part removed during refurbishment work conducted in 1995. Try and spot the remaining original tiles on the door's frame. Today, planned renovation includes refurbishing the façade and the addition of four storeys.

Nitza Metzger Scmuk

Sharon Golan Yaron

Sharon Golan Yaron

Sharon Golan Yaron

House Halpern

096 D

56 Shalma Street
[A] Alexander Penn
1937

Philipp Meuser

This building in the southern part of the city was built as a warehouse for a neighbouring zipper factory. The floor layout is arranged around a rectangular, open space with the gallery corridors overlooking it. Its relatively large dimensions are structured by the ribbon windows which gradually increase in height towards the top floor. The building extends along a main road and its centre part was designed to be opened in order to allow vehicle access from and to Salameh Street for shipping trucks. Today, the building is in an advanced state of derelict and has remained vacant for years. Since it is not listed as a protected monument and its function has become dispensable, its future is entirely unknown.

Philipp Meuser

Irmel Kamp-Bandau

Pivko Architects

House Honigman

097 D

60 Shalma Street
[A] Hillel Robert Chelouche
[R] Pivko Architects
1935

This building was commissioned by Lord Melchett, a wealthy British businessman, who, as a Zionist philanthropist, brought foreign investments into Mandate Palestine. The building served as a storage and administration facility for one of his chemical companies. The building was rapidly expanded during its first years, evolving from a single block to a U-shaped building complex. A steel-frame construction was installed on the ground floor in order to create maximum space for storage purposes, while the rest of the building served as office space. Despite being classified as an International Style building, its façade stands out for its Art Deco qualities. The staircase window located on the building's main façade features vertical ribbons made of steel and glass. For many years, the building accommodated Honigman, a local textile company after which the building is informally referred to. It also housed a bank branch, and the renowned Bezalel Academy's Master's programme. The building is planned to undergo massive renovation as part of an upcoming residential Florentine Square complex. The building project comprises 200 apartments of various sizes, 4,500 square metres of office space, and 2,300 square metres of commercial space. The units will be arranged around a U-shaped, 17-storey high-rise building, the highest in the new cityscape. Recently, the municipality agreed to a temporary us as an art gallery until the renovation work begins.

Philipp Meuser

Pivko Architects

Pivko Architects

Pivko Architects

Residential Building

098 D

85 Herzl Street
[A] Barzilay and Hausman
1935

Little is known regarding the history of this building. At the time of its construction, this part of Herzl Street was under the jurisdiction of the municipality of Jaffa and, as is true for many other buildings in this area, its documentation was lost during the Independence War of 1948. During the 1930s, the International Style was the *lingua franca* both in Jaffa and Tel Aviv. But while in Tel Aviv it was aspired to disconnect form former decorative styles, Jaffa's modernist buildings were designed with reference to the Art Deco style, explaining this building's unique façade. The building's clear symmetry hides a courtyard on the rear side, which is surrounded by the building's U-shaped footprint. Step inside and examine the black and white chequered flooring expanding from the entrance lobby towards the courtyard.

Philipp Meuser

Philipp Meuser

Philipp Meuser

ODO Architects

House Trevish

099 D

100 Herzl Street
[A] Eng. J Shapiro
[R] ODO Architects
1940s, 2017

Typologically, this building follows the principles of the International Style in the Florentin neighbourhood. Mixing residential and commercial functions, it is part of a block building. Central oriel windows characterise the façade, with balconies cantilevering over the sidewalk on both of its sides, as is a common feature of the buildings in the neighbourhood. The building's original owner was a butcher who operated a sausage factory located in the building's backyard. Despite not being listed as a monument, the building was renovated with an emphasis on its original form out of an understanding between the architect, the investor, and the municipality that its conservation would benefit the overall appeal and character of the neighbourhood. The renovation included the addition of two and a half additional storeys so that the building now comprises a total of seven floors. Further expansion included a gradual expansion towards the rear of the plot. The architects sought to emphasise the additions by using a contrasting material. In this case, the new parts are clad with HPL panels with a wood finish. The separation between old and the new makes it abundantly clear that this is a building that underwent renovation. To emphasise the new parts even further, orange glass adorns the new balconies.

Philipp Meuser

ODO Architects

Philipp Meuser

House Erlich 100 D

79 Herzl Street
[A] Zeev Haller
[R] Gal Peleg Architects
1933-1934

This building features curved lines as a tribute to the dynamics of the street intersection at which it is located, balconies with simple but elegant metal railings, and ribbon windows on each floor to emphasise the building's horizontality. A thermometer window extends across the height of the stairway, and the roof is adorned with a pergola. Designed by renowned German architect Zeev Haller, the building originally comprised three residential storeys above a ground floor that was used for commercially functions. The building's horizontality is enhanced by recessed ribbons clad with plaster that connect the window plane, and a band of narrow cornices that are coloured grey to contrast the white plaster covering the rest of the façade. The building underwent renovation in 2013, during which three additional storeys were added that comprised a total of seven apartments. The lower of the new storeys follows the original floorplan while the two uppermost storeys are recessed from the building's façade. During renovation, the building was also reinforced to withstand earthquakes. A unique aspect of this building is that the top balcony was shifted upwards: it was demolished only to be rebuilt on the floor above. A suitable solution for the challenging task of having to increase the height of a modernist building with subtle, horizontal proportions. We recommend taking a break in the neighbourhood café on the ground floor of the building.

Philipp Meuser

100 D

Amit Geron

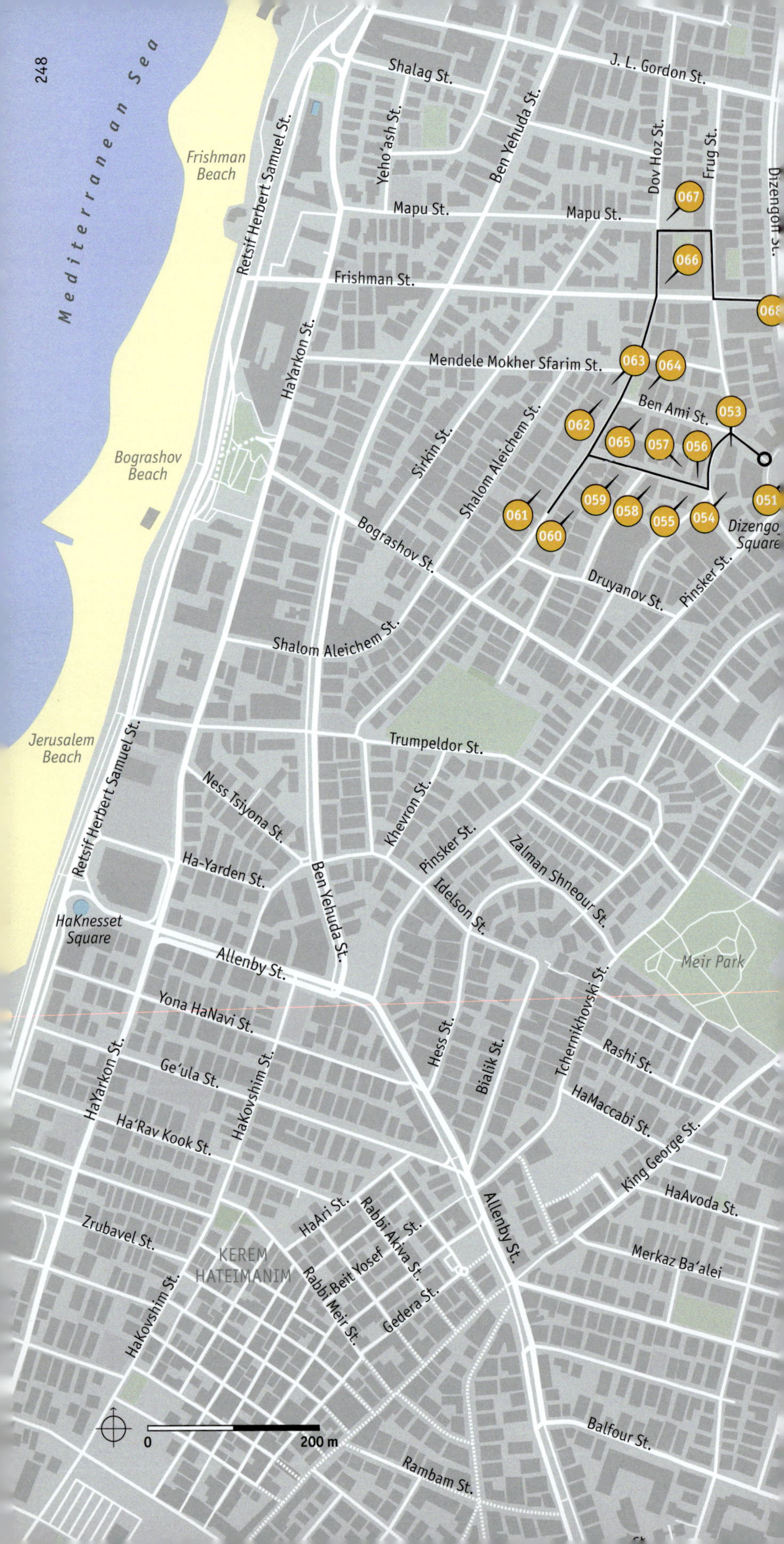
Mediterranean Sea
Frishman Beach
Bograshov Beach
Jerusalem Beach
HaKnesset Square
J. L. Gordon St.
Shalag St.
Yeho'ash St.
Ben Yehuda St.
Dov Hoz St.
Frug St.
Dizengoff St.
Mapu St.
Mapu St.
Retsif Herbert Samuel St.
Frishman St.
HaYarkon St.
Mendele Mokher Sfarim St.
Ben Ami St.
Sirkin St.
Shalom Aleichem St.
Bograshov St.
Dizengoff Square
Druyanov St.
Pinsker St.
Shalom Aleichem St.
Trumpeldor St.
Ness Tsiyona St.
Khevron St.
Pinsker St.
Zalman Shneour St.
Retsif Herbert Samuel St.
Ha-Yarden St.
Ben Yehuda St.
Idelson St.
Meir Park
Allenby St.
Tchernikhovski St.
Yona HaNavi St.
Hess St.
Bialik St.
Rashi St.
HaYarkon St.
Ge'ula St.
HaKovshim St.
HaMaccabi St.
Ha'Rav Kook St.
King George St.
HaAvoda St.
Zrubavel St.
HaAri St.
Rabbi Akiva St.
St.
Allenby St.
KEREM HATEIMANIM
Rabbi Beit Yosef
Rabbi Meir St.
Gedera St.
Merkaz Ba'alei
HaKovshim St.
0
200 m
Balfour St.
Rambam St.
067
066
068
063
064
053
062
065
057
056
061
059
058
055
054
051
060

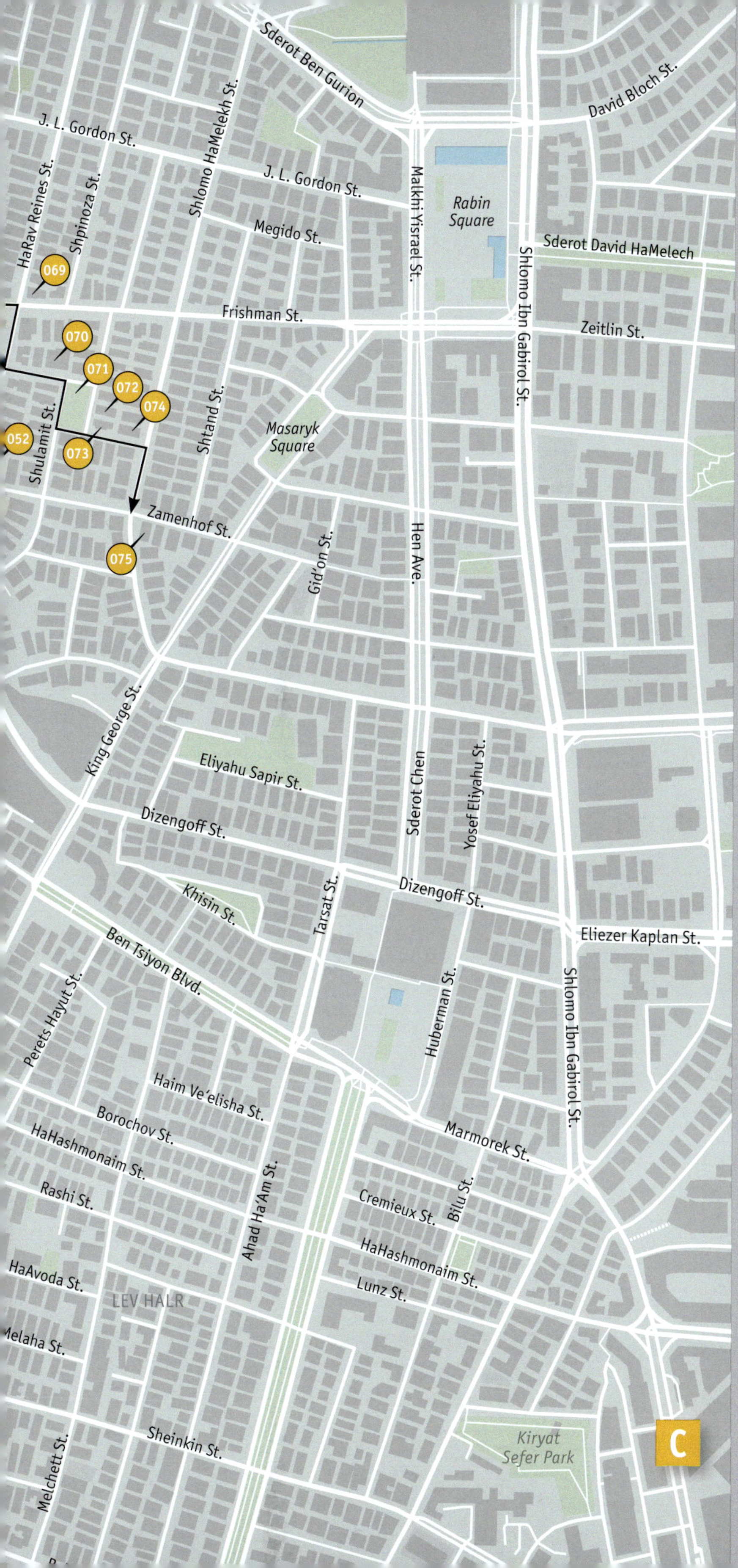
Sderot Ben Gurion
David Bloch St.
J. L. Gordon St.
J. L. Gordon St.
Shlomo HaMelekh St.
HaRav Reines St.
Shpinoza St.
Rabin Square
Malkhi Yisrael St.
Megido St.
Sderot David HaMelech
Shlomo Ibn Gabirol St.
069
Frishman St.
Zeitlin St.
070
071
072
074
052
073
Shulamit St.
Shtand St.
Masaryk Square
Zamenhof St.
075
Gid'on St.
Hen Ave.
King George St.
Eliyahu Sapir St.
Sderot Chen
Yosef Eliyahu St.
Dizengoff St.
Dizengoff St.
Tarsat St.
Khisin St.
Eliezer Kaplan St.
Ben Tsiyon Blvd.
Perets Hayut St.
Huberman St.
Shlomo Ibn Gabirol St.
Haim Ve'elisha St.
Marmorek St.
Borochov St.
HaHashmonaim St.
Ahad Ha'Am St.
Rashi St.
Cremieux St.
Bilu St.
HaHashmonaim St.
HaAvoda St.
Lunz St.
LEV HALR
Melaha St.
Sheinkin St.
Melchett St.
Kiryat Sefer Park
C

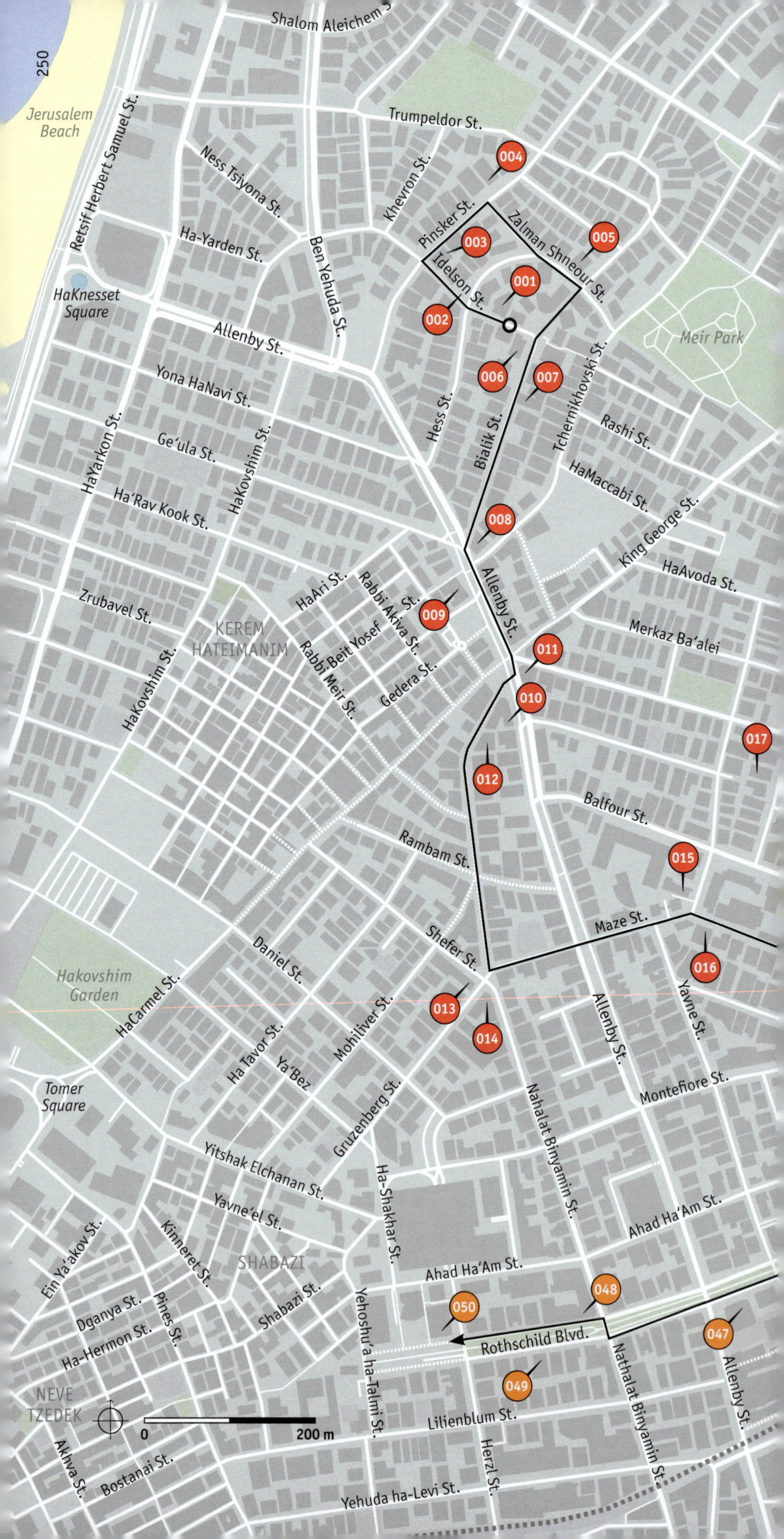
Shalom Aleichem St.
Jerusalem Beach
Trumpeldor St.
Retsif Herbert Samuel St.
Ness Tsiyona St.
Khevron St.
Pinsker St.
Zalman Shneour St.
Idelson St.
Ha-Yarden St.
Ben Yehuda St.
HaKnesset Square
Allenby St.
Meir Park
Yona HaNavi St.
Hess St.
Bialik St.
Tchernikhovski St.
Rashi St.
HaYarkon St.
Ge'ula St.
HaKovshim St.
HaMaccabi St.
Ha'Rav Kook St.
King George St.
HaAvoda St.
HaAri St.
Rabbi Akiva St.
Zrubavel St.
KEREM HATEIMANIM
Rabbi Beit Yosef St.
Merkaz Ba'alei
Rabbi Meir St.
Gedera St.
Balfour St.
Rambam St.
Maze St.
Shefer St.
Daniel St.
Hakovshim Garden
HaCarmel St.
Mohliver St.
Yavne St.
Ha Tavor St.
Ya'Bez
Nahalat Binyamin St.
Montefiore St.
Tomer Square
Gruzenberg St.
Yitshak Elchanan St.
Ha-Shakhar St.
Yavne'el St.
Ahad Ha'Am St.
Ein Ya'akov St.
Kinneret St.
SHABAZI
Shabazi St.
Yehoshu'a ha-Talmi St.
Dganya St.
Pines St.
Ha-Hermon St.
Rothschild Blvd.
NEVE TZEDEK
Lilienblum St.
Herzl St.
0
200 m
Akhva St.
Bostanai St.
Yehuda ha-Levi St.
001
002
003
004
005
006
007
008
009
010
011
012
013
014
015
016
017
047
048
049
050

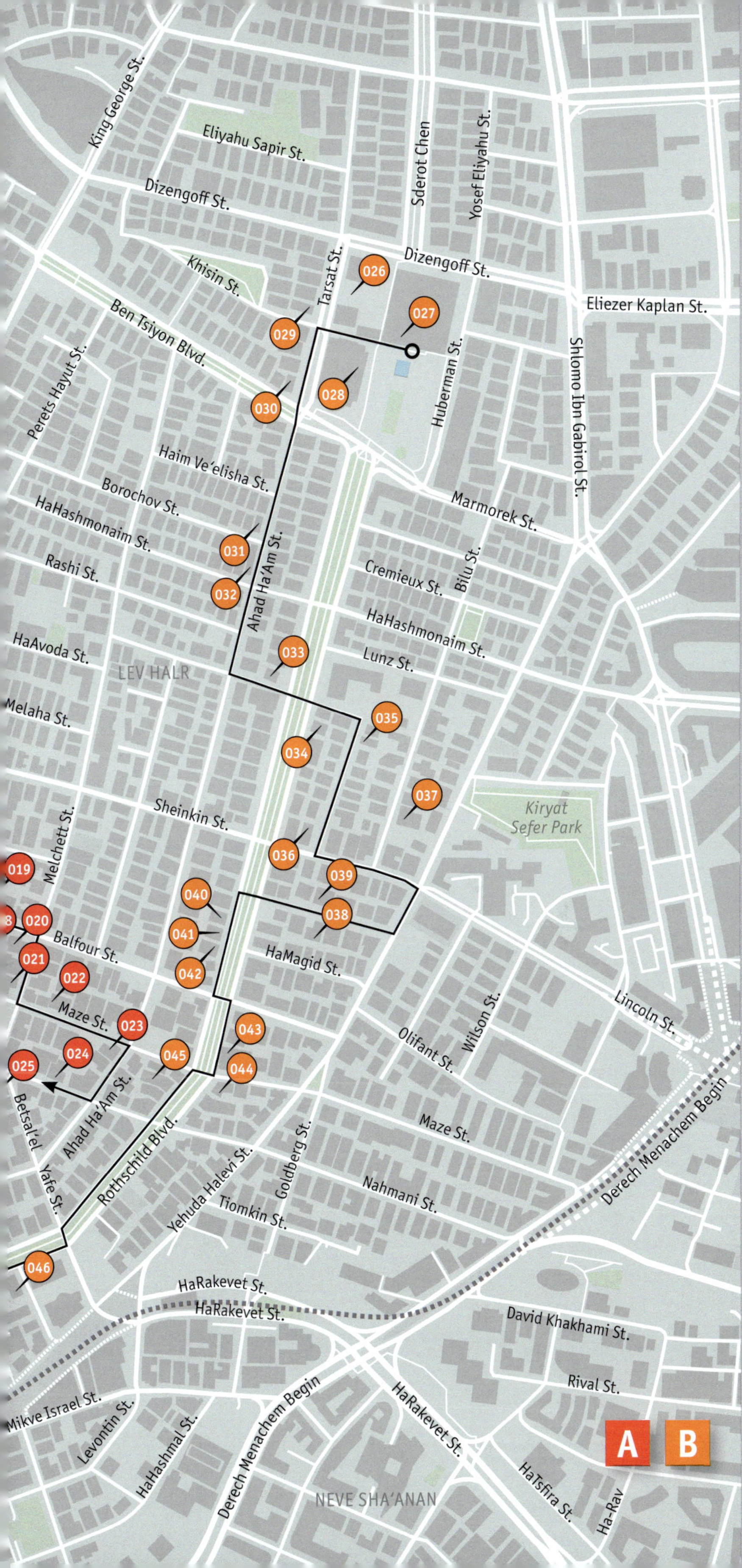
King George St.
Eliyahu Sapir St.
Dizengoff St.
Sderot Chen
Yosef Eliyahu St.
Dizengoff St.
Khisin St.
Tarsat St.
Eliezer Kaplan St.
Ben Tsiyon Blvd.
Perets Hayut St.
Huberman St.
Shlomo Ibn Gabirol St.
Haim Ve'elisha St.
Borochov St.
Marmorek St.
HaHashmonaim St.
Ahad Ha'Am St.
Rashi St.
Cremieux St.
Bilu St.
HaHashmonaim St.
HaAvoda St.
Lunz St.
LEV HA'IR
Melaha St.
Kiryat Sefer Park
Sheinkin St.
Melchett St.
Balfour St.
HaMagid St.
Maze St.
Lincoln St.
Olifant St.
Wilson St.
Ahad Ha'Am St.
Betsal'el Yafe St.
Rothschild Blvd.
Maze St.
Derech Menachem Begin
Yehuda Halevi St.
Goldberg St.
Nahmani St.
Tiomkin St.
HaRakevet St.
HaRakevet St.
David Khakhami St.
Rival St.
Mikve Israel St.
Levontin St.
HaHashmal St.
Derech Menachem Begin
HaRakevet St.
HaTsfira St.
Ha-Rav
NEVE SHA'ANAN
A
B
019
020
021
022
023
024
025
026
027
028
029
030
031
032
033
034
035
036
037
038
039
040
041
042
043
044
045
046

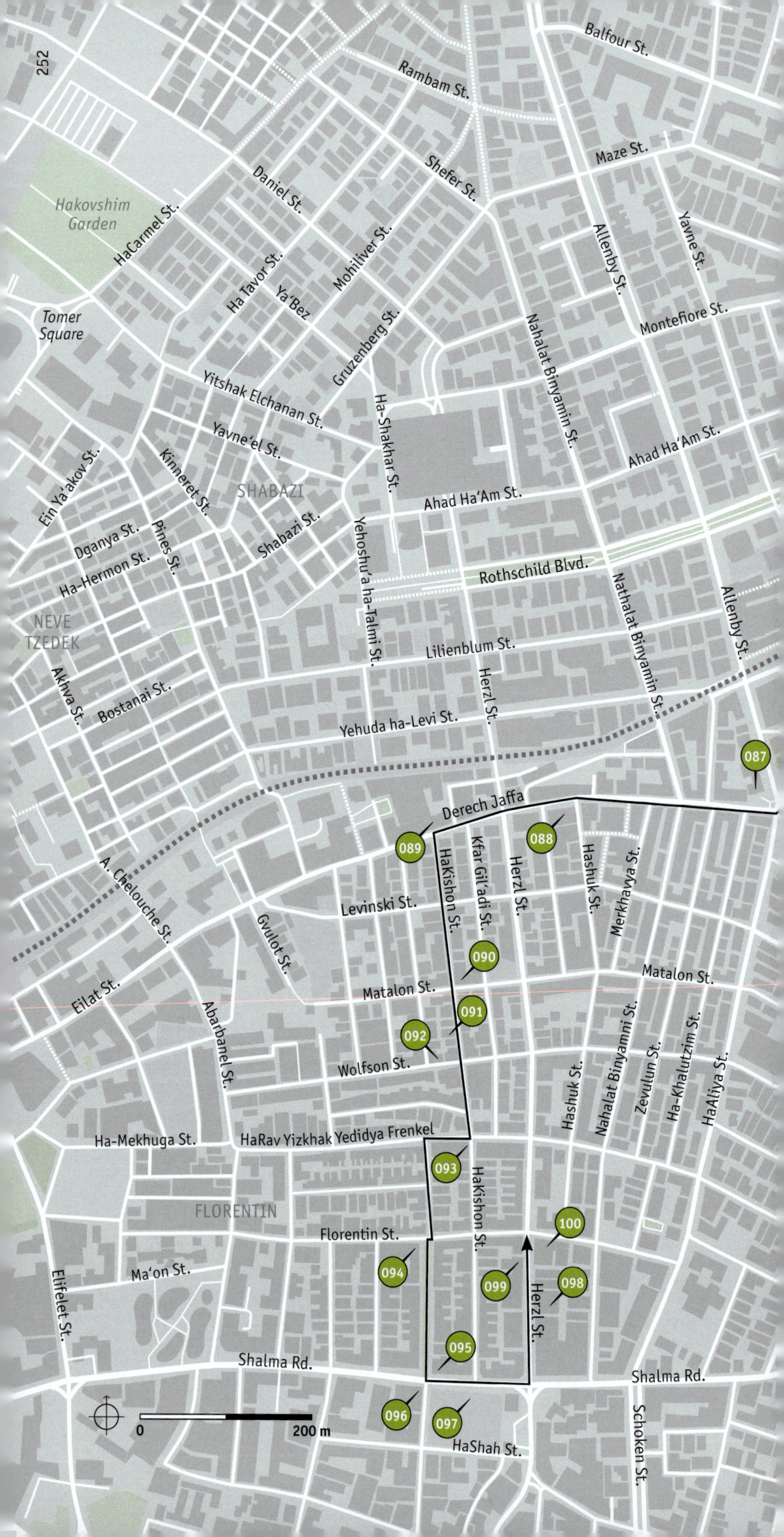

Balfour St.
Rambam St.
Maze St.
Shefer St.
Daniel St.
Hakovshim Garden
HaCarmel St.
Yavne St.
Allenby St.
Mohiliver St.
HaTavor St.
Ya'Bez
Tomer Square
Montefiore St.
Gruzenberg St.
Nahalat Binyamin St.
Yitshak Elchanan St.
Ha-Shakhar St.
Yavne'el St.
Ahad Ha'Am St.
Ein Ya'akov St.
Kinneret St.
SHABAZI
Ahad Ha'Am St.
Shabazi St.
Dganya St.
Pines St.
Yehoshu'a ha-Talmi St.
Ha-Hermon St.
Rothschild Blvd.
Nathalat Binyamin St.
Allenby St.
NEVE TZEDEK
Lilienblum St.
Akhva St.
Bostanai St.
Herzl St.
Yehuda ha-Levi St.
087
Derech Jaffa
088
089
Hakishon St.
Kfar Gil'adi St.
Herzl St.
Hashuk St.
Merkhavya St.
A. Chelouche St.
Levinski St.
Gvulot St.
090
Matalon St.
Eilat St.
Matalon St.
091
Abarbanel St.
092
Wolfson St.
Hashuk St.
Nahalat Binyamni St.
Zevulun St.
Ha-Khalutzim St.
HaAliya St.
Ha-Mekhuga St.
HaRav Yizkhak Yedidya Frenkel
093
HaKishon St.
FLORENTIN
100
Florentin St.
Ma'on St.
094
099
098
Herzl St.
Elifelet St.
095
Shalma Rd.
Shalma Rd.
096
097
0
200 m
HaShah St.
Schoken St.

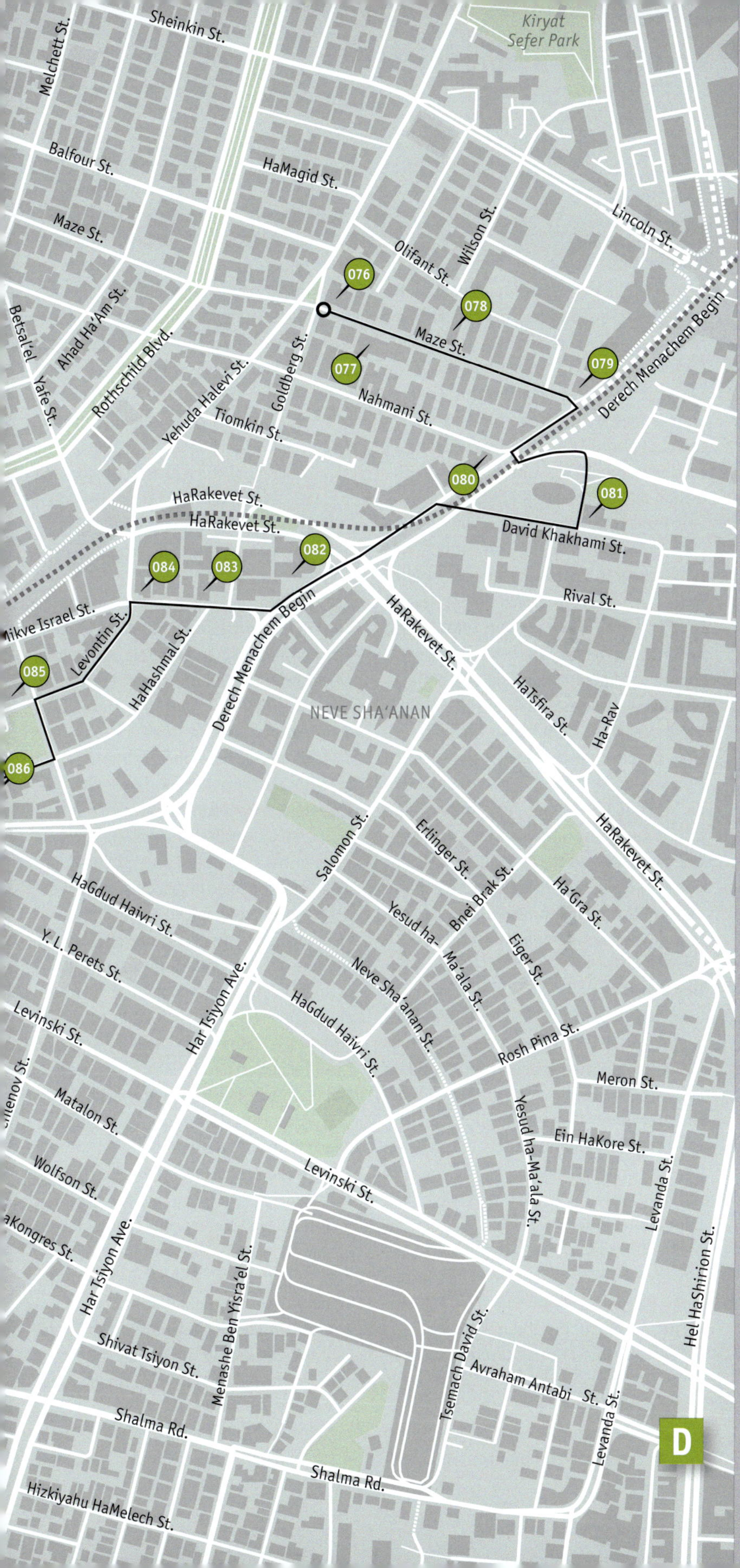
Kiryat Sefer Park
Sheinkin St.
Melchett St.
Balfour St.
HaMagid St.
Maze St.
Lincoln St.
Wilson St.
Olifant St.
076
078
077
079
Maze St.
Derech Menachem Begin
Ahad Ha'Am St.
Betsal'el Yafe St.
Rothschild Blvd.
Yehuda Halevi St.
Goldberg St.
Nahmani St.
Tiomkin St.
080
081
HaRakevet St.
HaRakevet St.
David Khakhami St.
082
084
083
Rival St.
Mikve Israel St.
Levontin St.
HaHashmal St.
Derech Menachem Begin
HaRakevet St.
085
HaTsfira St.
Ha-Rav
NEVE SHA'ANAN
086
Salomon St.
Erlinger St.
HaRakevet St.
HaGdud Haivri St.
Bnei Brak St.
Ha'Gra St.
Yesud ha-Ma'ala St.
Y. L. Perets St.
Har Tsiyon Ave.
Neve Sha'anan St.
Eiger St.
Levinski St.
HaGdud Haivri St.
Rosh Pina St.
Meron St.
Matalon St.
Yesud ha-Ma'ala St.
Ein HaKore St.
Wolfson St.
Levinski St.
Levanda St.
HaKongres St.
Har Tsiyon Ave.
Menashe Ben Yisra'el St.
Hel HaShirion St.
Shivat Tsiyon St.
Tsemach David St.
Avraham Antabi St.
Shalma Rd.
Levanda St.
D
Shalma Rd.
Hizkiyahu HaMelech St.

Architects' Biographies

Arieh Sharon

Israel's most important Bauhaus architect Arieh Sharon was born in Poland. He was one of the founders of Kibbutz Givat Shmuel, which sent him to study architecture in Germany. Sharon studied at the Bauhaus in Dessau under Walter Gropius and Hannes Meyer. Upon his return from the Bauhaus to Tel Aviv, he established an architectural office, specialising in the design of residential buildings. One of his first project was the Cooperative Housing Estate Hod built in 1935 (see tour 3). In Israel, Sharon designed numerous buildings, from residential apartment houses to communal buildings in rural areas, hospitals, cinemas, and many others. All together he planned around 600 projects of which half were actually built. Sharon's most important work began when Israel's first prime minister, David Ben-Gurion, commissioned him in 1949 to lead the national team for the first master plan in the newly established State of Israel. Literally meaning that a Bauhaus student not only designed residential housing in Tel Aviv but was also responsible for the strategic planning for all of Israel.

Dov Karmi

Born in Odessa in 1905, Dov Karmi emigrated to Palestine in 1921. He studied at the Bezalel Academy in Jerusalem and later in Ghent, Belgium. At the time, Henry van de Velde (known as a driving force of Modernism, he became the head of Grand-Ducal Saxonian School of Arts and Crafts in Weimar, from which the Bauhaus emerged in 1919) was Professor of Architecture and Applied Arts at the university (1925-1936). Upon his return from Belgium, Karmi founded his own office, Madben, together with Eng. Zvi Barak. Amongst others, Karmi influenced the shift to Modernism in Israel and was one of the founders of the Israeli circle of architects, the Chug. He designed around two hundred buildings, including cultural facilities, public buildings, apartment buildings and private houses in Tel Aviv. His work was regarded as exemplary and granted him nationwide recognition. Well-known for his understanding of subtle detailing, he was awarded the Israel Prize for Architecture, the first recipient of the prize in his field. Among his masterpieces is the Max-Liebling House (see tour 1), home of the White City Centre. In his later career he shifted toward building in the brutalist style, marking the turning point towards this style in Israel.

Zeev Rechter

Born in Kovalivka in Ukraine in 1899, Zeev Rechter migrated to Israel in 1919 where he worked in a Kibbutz and at the Jewish Agency. In 1926, he went to Rome to study architecture, and in 1927 he designed a residence for the poet Esther Raab in an early modernist style, inspired by his impressions from Italy. Unfortunately, the house was later demolished. In 1929, he went to the École des Ponts et Chaussées in Paris to continue his studies. It was here that he became an enthusiastic disciple of Le Corbusier. Upon his return to Tel Aviv he was one of the founders of the Chug group of architects. Rechter was the first to use *piloti* (concrete pillars) for his houses in Israel (see House Engel, tour 2), which in the later period of the 1930s became a typical feature of the local Modernism.

Zeev (Wilhelm) Haller

Zeev Haller, born in 1884 in Leipzig, Germany, was a very highly regarded architect even before his emigration to Palestine in 1932. He developed a unique new "Jewish Style" when building for the Leipzig Jewish community that incorporated abstract, gothic elements and Moorish motifs. Unfortunately, all of his significant buildings in Germany were destroyed. Because of the strict municipal regulations in Palestine forcing to build in the modernistic style, his buildings evolved from Expressionism into a style of articulated Minimalism created with his own, very particular signature. This style involved a dynamic expression of architecture, for example by segmenting the façade into wave-shaped elements (see House Bruno, tour 1).

Yitzchak Rapoport
Born in Ukraine in 1901 and emigrated to Palestine in 1914, Yitzchak Rapoport studied at the Technical University in Berlin and then at the Ecole Spéciale des Travaux Publics in Paris. Upon his return to Palestine, he worked for the British mandate power. After working with one of the country's leading modernist architects, Richard Kauffmann, he opened his own architectural office in 1932. Among his famous buildings is the recently renovated House Aharonovitch (see tour 2).

Carl Rubin
Born in 1899 in Galicia, Poland, Carl Rubin studied architecture in Vienna before emigrating to Palestine in 1920. In 1931, he went to Berlin to work for Erich Mendelsohn, and one year later opened an office in Tel Aviv. One of Rubin's most important designs is the building that, today, is Israel's famous Independence Hall (16 Rothschild Boulevard) after serving as the home of Tel Aviv's first Mayor Meir Dizengoff, who donated it to the city to turn it into an art museum. In 1935, Rubin designed the Beit Hadar office building (see tour 2), the first building in Tel Aviv with a steel frame structure.

Jaakov (Ben Sira) Shiffman
Shiffman was Tel Aviv's city architect for 21 years, from 1929 to 1950. Originally from Ukraine, he graduated from engineering studies in London. His influence on the modernistic building style in Tel Aviv was immense, since he ordered that the Eclectic Style was to be abandoned in all of Tel Aviv and enforced building in the International Style only. During his time as city architect, he was not only responsible for the construction of the Tel Aviv Port and the Tel Aviv Promenade, but many other public buildings and sites, as well. These include a series of innovative schools and the building for the medical emergency service House Magen David Adom (see tour 2).

Richard Kauffmann
Richard Kauffman was the earliest and most influential modernist architect in Israel. Born in Frankfurt, Germany, in 1887, he graduated in urban engineering from Technical University Munich and, in 1919, connected with the leading planner of the Zionist development organisation, Arthur Ruppin. Ruppin invited him to design new Jewish settlements in Palestine at a time when he was still working as a governmental town planner in Christiania, now Oslo, Norway. As the chief architect of the Palestine Land Development Company (PLDC), Kauffmann designed architectural master plans for new kibbutzim and moshavim in the northern valleys, most notably Ein Harod, Kfar Yehoshua, Degania Alef, Kfar Yehezkel and Nahalal. He conceptualised cities like Afula and Herzliya and developed the first plan for Tel Aviv and many residential neighbourhoods around the country. He had a private office in an old windmill in Jerusalem from where he also planned numerous private buildings. His architectural legacy is perhaps the largest of the country, with numerous buildings that were decidedly modern and ahead of their time. House Kruksal house (see tour 1) is the earliest modernistic building in Tel Aviv that still stands today.

Oskar Kaufman
Oskar Kaufmann, born in 1873, was perhaps the most well-known German theatre architect of his time. He designed numerous theatres, opera houses and

concert halls, amongst which the Kroll Oper, Hebbel Theater, and the Renaissance Theatre, all in Berlin, as well as the Neue Stadttheater in Vienna. He created most of his theatre buildings in Berlin during the 1920s. In addition, Kaufmann designed a number of villas for affluent owners. In 1928, art critic Max Osborn invented the term Expressionist Rococo to describe Kaufmann's work. Kaufmann immigrated to Israel in 1934, where he had been asked to plan the Habima National Theatre (see tour 2). However, the young and still inexperienced architects who determined the building scene in Israel at the time had reservation against Kaufmann. The lack of European cultural norms and the harsh economic conditions prevailing in the country at the time caused Kaufmann to leave Israel the before the Habima Theatre was completed; his partner Eugen Stolzer supervised the completion. During his stay in Israel, Kaufmann built only a few other buildings, the only one in Tel Aviv being House Dunkelblum (see tour 3). Although Kauffman's style was originally "baroque", featuring detailed ornaments, he adapted to the minimalist style broadly accepted in Israel. However, his own unique modernistic style integrating details that reflect his rich, virtuously applied knowledge of theatre design.

Josef Neufeld

Josef Neufeld was born in 1898 in Ukraine. After studying at the Academy of Art in Vienna and the Accademia delle Belle Arti in Rome, he worked for some of the leading German architects such as Erich Mendelsohn in Berlin and Bruno Taut in Moscow. In 1932, Neufeld opened an office in Tel Aviv, where he built residential houses, hospitals, schools, and cooperative housing estates. He was a member of the architecture circle Chug. Among his most distinguished works is the Former Health Administration Center Kupat Cholim Clalit, which won a prize for its functional design (see tour 3). The centre is one of only few public buildings built in Tel Aviv in that time. In the 1940s, Neufeld moved to the United States where he was Professor of Architectural Design at Yale University.

Pinchas (Philip) Hütt

Pinchas (Philip) Hütt was born in Lviv, Ukraine, in 1888. He studied in Chernivtsi, Bucovina, and attended classes at the Bauhaus school in Weimar because the approach taught there appealed to him. In Tel Aviv, where he designed many buildings, he opened his own office. Among them were House Mintz-Elenberg (see tour 1) and House Minzer (see tour 2), a boarding house for young women. In 1928, he planned the Levant Fair. His first buildings were designed in the Eclectic Style, and only later turned to the International Style. Toward the end of his professional career, Huett served as city architect for the municipality of Tel Aviv.

Leo Adler

Leo Adler was a well-known German architect, architectural theorist, architectural critic, and author ("Lexikon der Baukunst"). He was a member of Deutscher Werkbund and the Association of German Architects. Born in Russia in 1891, he began studying architecture at the Technical University of Berlin and, in 1912, went to Munich to continue his studies. After graduating, he was deployed in the First World War, and was badly wounded. Leo Adler received his doctorate in 1920 from Cornelius Gurlitt at the Dresden University of Technology. After he was arrested by the Nazis in 1933 he decided to flee to Palestine. He only realised five buildings in Israel, among them House Romanov (1925), which today houses the boutique hotel Norman (see tour 2) and marks the shift from the eclectic to the modern style of building. He also worked as editor of the architectural journal Habinjan Bamisrach Hakarov (Building in the Near East) and acted as chief architect of the Gilboa region in northern Israel from 1955 to 1958.

Genia Averbuch

In Palestine of the 1930s, female architects where part of the establishment, both in design and in building. Born in 1909, Genia Averbuch was an immigrant who came to Palestine from Russia when she was only 17 years old. She went to study architecture in the Regia Scuola di Architettura in Rome and then continued her studies in Belgium where, in 1930, she received a diploma in architecture from the Royal Academy of Arts of Brussels. Averbuch returned to Palestine and launched her professional career at the age of 21. She worked with Richard Kauffmann and designed numerous apartment buildings and urban villas. Together with Elsa Gidoni Mandelstamm she designed Café Galina for the Levant Fair in 1934. In the same year, Averbuch won a competition for the design of a municipal square in Tel Aviv's most prominent urban sites, the Dizengoff Square (see tour 3). She also designed several buildings around the square, which still symbolises the heart of the White City.

Sam Barkay

Born in Russia in 1898, Sam Barkay first studied in Venice at the Acadamia delle Belle Arti and then in Paris at the École Nationale Supérieure des Beaux-Arts. Working at Le Corbusier's studio tremendously influenced Barkay's architectural language. Upon his return to Palestine, he started working for the Bohemian Society of Israel, for whom he mostly built residential buildings, for example House Aginski (see tour 2). He joined the architects' association Chug and was one of the first reporters for the Chug's journal. He has also reported on young Israeli architecture in the journal L'Architecture d'Aujourd'hui, contributing significantly to the international awareness of modern building in Israel.

Erich Mendelsohn

German architect Erich Mendelsohn was one of the greatest influencers on the formation of local Modernism in Israel. In Germany, he was already well-known for his dynamic Functionalism, which coined projects such as the Einstein Tower, numerous department stores, and many other buildings before he emigrated to Palestine in 1934 due to the antisemitism in Nazi Germany. With his architectural language, Mendelsohn responded to local building traditions, which can mainly to be seen in his buildings outside of Tel Aviv. In the White City, his greatest influence were the rounded balconies as streamline elements – a feature that was copied by many other architects in the region although Mendelsohn himself was rather reluctant about the implementation of his design language in the city. Only one building in Tel Aviv was actually planned by his office, the Max Fein Technical School (see tour 2).

Zaki Chelouche

Born in Jaffa in 1894, Zaki Chelouche was the descendant of an elite Sephardic (diaspora of Jews from Arabic states) family and founders of Achuzat Beit, the first Tel Aviv neighbourhood. Upon returning from his studies in France in 1928, he designed residential buildings that embodied both Art Deco and International Style elements (see House Barun, tour 1). If there is a consensus regarding the International Style in Tel Aviv being connected to the Ashkenazim (Jews of european background), Chelouche and other architects from Sephardic background prove us wrong.

Yael Schmidt

Yael Schmidt

Yael Schmidt

Index of Architects

Index of Buildings

Index of Streets

Yael Schmidt

Yael Schmidt

Yael Schmidt

dpa picture alliance / Alamy Stock Photo

Yael Schmidt

Yael Schmidt

Yael Schmidt

Yael Schmidt

The Author

Sharon Golan Yaron
is a conservation architect and the Program Director of the White City Centre. During her work at the municipality of Tel Aviv Jaffa, she laid the foundation and co-founded the White City Centre in the *Max-Liebling House* – a joint project of the municipality of Tel Aviv Jaffa and the German Federal Ministry of Building. She studied Architecture at the IIT Chicago and the TU Belin, followed by a master degree in architectural conservation at the Technion of Haifa.

Acknowledgements/Thanks to

Irmel Kamp-Bandau for her pictures taken in the white city in the 1980s
Nitza Metzger Szmuk for her help in defining the tours and for the help with the historical pictures
Tamara Garon for her help in designing the outline of the tours
Shira Beneymini Levi for helping with the editing of the text
Hadas Nevo Goldberst for editing the second tour
Shula Widerich for helping with pictures
Rinat Milo for editing the fourth tour
Zvi Efrat for help with historical pictures
Wendy Gordon for her help with editing the English text
Gil Yaron my dear husband and best mentor ever

Historic photographs by:
Itzhak Kalter
Zoltan Kluger
Kurt Bremer

Archives and collections:
Albert Sqr. image
Courtesy of the Department of Special Collections, Stanford Libraries
Photos from the Matson (G. Eric and Edith) Photograph Collection
Drawings from Tel Aviv's Municipal Archive
Library of Congress

The Deutsche Bibliothek lists this publication in the Deutsche Nationalbibliografie; detailed bibliographic data is available @ dnb.d-nb.de

DOM publishers

ISBN 978-3-86922-252-3 (English)
ISBN 978-3-86922-268-4 (German)

Proofreading
Usch Engelmann

Translation (German)
Daniela Pogade

Design
Cristina Montellano

QR-Codes
Christoph Gößmann

Maps
Katrin Soschinski

Printing
Master Print Super Offset S.R.L., Bucharest
www.masterprint.ro

Partners

בית ליבלינג LIEBLING HAUS

Tel Aviv Yafo Foundation

מוסדות חינוך ותרבות בתל אביב יפו

Federal Ministry of the Interior, Building and Community

TEL AVIV YAFO תל אביב יפו